Introductions

BY

STEVE GLASSON

&

ROBBIE DOBBINS

ROLLED GOLD

ROLLED GOLD

THE KELVIN KERKOW STORY

KELVIN KERKOW

WITH DAVID TENENBAUM

M

MELBOURNE BOOKS

Published by Melbourne Books
Level 9, 100 Collins Street,
Melbourne, VIC, 3000
Australia

www.melbournebooks.com.au
info@melbournebooks.com.au

Photos provided from the private collection of Kelvin
Kerkow with thanks to Paul Grant, Nationwide Bowler
magazine and Melvyn Beck, Bowls International magazine
Any person who believes they have not been properly
attributed may contact the publisher for correction in any
future printing.
National Library of Australia Cataloguing-in-
Publication entry
Author: Kerkow, Kelvin.
Title: Rolled Gold: The Kelvin Kerkow Story
Kelvin Kerkow.
ISBN: 9781877096907 (pbk.)
Subjects: Kerkow, Kelvin.
Lawn bowls-Australia-Biography.
Other Authors: Tenenbaum, David.
Dewey Number: 796.315092

Front cover photo: Paul Harris FAIRFAXPHOTOS.COM
Back cover photo: David Holman www.fotoforce.com

I dedicate this book to my beautiful wife Karen,
my two boys Kirk and Ky and also
a big thank you to my Mum and Dad.
All the hard times have been worth it.

The year is 1985 and it's round 1 of the Queensland Junior Singles Championships at the Pine Rivers Memorial Bowls Club in the northern suburbs of Brisbane.

This junior event, the pinnacle of junior bowls tournaments in Queensland, mainly due to the fact that it was basically the only one, featured singles play in a knock-out format played, for the best part, over a week, being timed to fit around other local and club events at the then tiny Pine Rivers Club.

With nerves at an all time high, my late father, Bob Glasson, himself a Queensland representative, drives me to the venue on the other side of Brisbane, offering me all types of sound advice and wisdom. Round 1 comes and goes and he stays to watch, risking trouble from his bosses but willing to take the punt!

Alas, success in the opening encounters! Phew, that settles the nerves a bit and brings on some confidence!

My father approaches me at lunch time and congratulates me on winning my first round. He offers more advice but then says something that has always stuck in my head. He states, 'Steve, if you are going to win this title, the young man sitting over there, is the one to beat!' He is pointing at fellow junior, unknown to us all, one Kelvin Ivan Kerkow.

As luck would have it, we meet in the final and on this occasion, it happened to fall my way however who would have guessed that this meeting would be the first of so many that I can't even begin to remember.... hundreds anyway!

More importantly, it was the first time I met this most remarkable person. At our first meeting, Kelvin never used his customary stick, he did however brandish a lovely pair of old brown bowls shoes and covered his trademark flat-top haircut with a little cream bowlers peaked cap. Of course, he still has the flat-top but gone are those shoes and cap.

Since this meeting some 25 years ago, I am honoured that Kelvin (or otherwise known as Jug Head, Flat-top, Spike or in more recent times No.43) has become my nearest and dearest friend.

As an example, we are God parents to each other's children. We have toured domestically and internationally so many, many times. In fact, for a number of years I think we lived together more than we did with our own families!

As with any successful sports-person, there are always the highs however with these highs, sometimes from completely nowhere, there are the lows too.

Over the years, Kelvin and I have shared both of these emotions! Kelvin's record on the green speaks for itself and he will already be deemed as one of the greatest bowlers, if not **the** best, to have been produced on Australian shores. I'm sure we will be privy to much more success from this super talented competitor for many years to come. Strangely enough, he classes himself a better fisherman than bowler. I'm not so sure about that!

Of course, it's easy to accept, enjoy and embrace success. It's when it comes to the tough times that one's true character really comes to the fore. I know for a fact that one of Kelvin's greatest disappointments was being omitted from the Australian Commonwealth Games Team for the 1998 Malaysia (KL) Games. This really deflated him however, as he has proven in his already tough life, he bounced back and history will show and celebrate his greatest victory, the Commonwealth Games Gold Medal in the blue ribbon singles event in Melbourne in 2006.

Kelvin has taken setbacks in his stride (although there have been few of these on the green) and in addition to that, he has also proven to be a great confidant and true friend when I have suffered disappointments in my career!

He has always spoken openly and honestly, he talks straight from the heart and is a fantastic member of a team! Of course, he has had great support from his family over the years, no more so than from his parents Ivan & Joan and also wife Karen & sons, Kirk and Ky.

Mind you, he's not perfect…that's why I would never suggest that anybody gets in a car with him when he's driving. Ha ha! It's always a white knuckle trip with him talking on the phone while eating and steering with his knees!

Kelvin's greatest victory however has of course been his victory over the dreaded childhood disease, Guillain-Barré Syndrom, a form of Polio! It took Kelvin years to recover from an overnight debilitating attack on his body and even to this day, he still suffers from this disease and that is why he walks with a limp and still uses his walking stick.

Kelvin is admired for his achievements and he is a world wide celebrity. He is a loving husband who adores his family and he brandishes a great easy going nature with a cheeky and dry sense of humour.

He has proven to me on so many occasions to be an inspiration both on and off the green with the way he approaches life and bowls. He has a highly competitive nature with an uncanny knack of being at his absolute best when his back is against the wall.

At the time of writing this, we still travel regularly together for bowls, with most of our efforts now focussed on the PBA series in the UK. Not only that but we also work together for BCiB, (Bowling Club Insurance Brokers), a company that works with bowling clubs across Australia in risk management.

I personally wish him every success in all that he aspires to and I no doubt have all the confidence in the world that he will prove to be a success in whatever he turns his hands to.

I'm sure you will enjoy this book and appreciate all that Kelvin has had to endure on his way to ultimate success. You will certainly gain an insiders look at what he has gone through and what goes on 'behind the scenes' in the world of bowls!

Steve Glasson 2009

I suppose when people speak of 'heroes' they talk about a select few who venture beyond what others would expect them to accomplish, and struggle against great odds and setbacks to win great victories. I class Kelvin Kerkow in this category.

I first met Kelvin just after his 17th birthday, when he knocked on my door at Tweed Heads and asked if he joined Coolangatta Bowls Club of which I was a member, would I play with and coach him in this great game of Lawn Bowls.

He had previously been playing at the rather small Palm Beach Currumbin bowls club and wished to improve his game.

Kelvin at that time was a very lean boy who had a limp which was an after effect of the serious illness, Guillain-Barré Syndrome, and he needed a walking stick to support his leg and steady his balance when he bowled.

During the following years I would like a dollar for every person who commented that the stick was an advantage to his skill level. My stock reply was always the same, 'Kelvin will swap you the stick and his bad leg for your good leg any time you're ready.'

Since that knock on my door back in 1986, I have had the pleasure of being a mentor for Kelvin and was a team-mate when he won his first District, State, and Australian Titles. We were together when he won his first Australian fours title and then two days later was his coach/manager when he represented Australian in the Trans Tasman test series in NZ.

Kelvin is a person who has no fear and will try anything.

When managing the Australian men's team at World Bowls in Adelaide in 1996, Kelvin won two World Bowls Bronze Medals.

A newspaper reporter asked me prior to the start of the event if any of the bowlers would do a bungy jump in the city. He explained that he was looking for something which would alter the perception the public had, that Lawn Bowls was an old person's sport.

My reply, after questioning him as to the safety of this media ploy was, 'I can only think of one person who might try this escapade'. So off we went and asked Kelvin if he was interested. His reply was, 'bring it on, piece of cake, I'm your man.'

We have been white water rafting in New Zealand on a day when all other rafting tour operators called off the day's events as heavy overnight rain upstream was a consideration the river could be too dangerous. When we arrived at the river the water was a boiling mass of white water, and the guide remarked that, 'maybe we shouldn't go'. However after some 'no problem,' encouragement from Kelvin, we set out.

Kelvin and I were positioned in the front of the raft as we set off down the raging rapids. The water was so wild, that as we entered a grade 5 rapid, we lost the guide over the back, and

Rex Johnston over the side. We finally dragged Rex back in over the side, spluttering water and looking like a drowned cat.

I have watched over 21 years this small, frail, shy boy, grow into a fine family man and a great ambassador for the game of bowls and the country he represents.

During these years of our friendship we have travelled a lot of miles together, bowling, fishing, adventuring, and occasionally partying and celebrating.

On a personal level, I'm proud and honored to call Kelvin Kerkow my friend, colleague, and mate.

ROBBIE DOBBINS 2009

My Story

1

Rolled Gold

Friday, 24 March 2006. A capacity crowd filled the Darebin International Sports Centre, the stadium in Melbourne's northern suburbs purpose-built for the 2006 Commonwealth Games. At night, under floodlights, the atmosphere was tense as two thousand fans held their breath and willed me on.

Down an end and a shot in the best-of-three ends sudden-death playoff for the men's singles gold medal at the 2006 Commonwealth Games, to say I was under pressure would be an understatement. My opponent, the world number seven Robert Weale from Wales, playing in his sixth Commonwealth Games, held shot with his bowl less than a foot from the jack. I had one bowl left to play. I stood on the mat and surveyed my options and said to myself, 'I can draw this.'

I took a moment to decide which shot to play. One mistake and it was all over. I'd have the silver but I'd come for gold. I could play right through the head and take his bowl out or dead draw the shot. Weale's shot bowl sat at two o'clock and I felt there was enough room to sneak past it, so I played a forehand draw.

The bowl felt smooth out of my hand and I immediately thought I had drawn the shot, but as it approached the head it began to slow. The greens at Darebin had been crafted especially for the Games and were slower than we are accustomed to in Australia. Combined with the night dew, what would normally have been a 'toucher' was beginning to look like it might not have the legs.

I chased it all the way down the green. Most of the way I was confident I had stolen the shot but in the last metre it stopped so quickly that my confidence turned to anxiety. 'Is it going to get there?' I asked myself.

My bowl rolled to a stop at what appeared to be the same distance from the jack as Weale's bowl. It was too close for either one of us or the marker to call. It was now up to the umpire and his tape measure. My heart was in my mouth. The crowd was silent. The umpire measured, then rolled my bowl away to indicate that I held the shot — by three millimetres! The crowd roared. It was one-all with one end to play: win this end, win the gold.

I took a brief time-out to be right in the moment and appreciate the enormity of this last end I was about to play, and to reflect on how far I had come to get to this point. In fact, at an earlier point in my life, it looked like I may never walk again, let alone win a Commonwealth Games gold medal.

Lemons

I felt like I was almost weightless as I sprinted on the track my father had laid using old sump oil on the back paddock on my family's 320 acre peanut farm. I was eight years old and had not a care in the world and was looking forward to the 200 metre under-ten district championships, for which I had recently qualified. I was the quickest in my age group in my little area comprising a couple of schools in my corner of the world in rural Queensland at Wooroolin, about 230kms west of Brisbane.

The following morning, I complained of sore calf muscles, but dismissed the soreness as probably being related to running too hard. But that night I also started to feel pain in my hands and had trouble holding my cutlery at dinner. My parents didn't think it was anything to be concerned about — just growing pains. But that all changed dramatically when I woke in the middle of the night. I needed to go to the toilet, but when I tried to get out of bed I was unable to move my legs.

It was scary. Out in the country in the middle of the night it is pitch black. I couldn't move and I didn't know what was going on. I cried out to my parents. They came running and immediately knew something was wrong. I wasn't the kind of kid to fake something like that.

When my dad picked me up to take me to the doctor, my body was like a lump of jelly. He carried me to the car and rushed me to Wondai Hospital, a trip of about 25 minutes.

I was met at the hospital by the Head Sister, Olive Kiehne who advised that the doctor would be there shortly. We waited for four hours until Dr Kirkman arrived at 8am. In an incredible stroke of luck, the relieving doctor on duty had seen my symptoms in a patient before and ordered that I be rushed by ambulance to the Royal Children's Hospital in Brisbane.

I had contracted the very rare Guillain-Barré syndrome, an air-borne virus that was even rarer in country Queensland in 1978. Guillain-Barré syndrome is a disorder in which the body's immune system attacks part of the peripheral nervous system, increasing in intensity until certain muscles cannot be used at all. In severe cases, the patient is almost totally paralysed, and I was fast moving down that track. It meant my life was in danger because in these cases the disorder can interfere with breathing, blood pressure and heart rate.

It was almost divine intervention that the regular Wondai doctor was away that night. If the relieving English doctor had not diagnosed my condition, I probably wouldn't have lasted the night.

Mum arranged for Dad's parents to look after my two younger sisters, Katrina and Bronwyn, before the ambulance picked her up in Wooroolin for the three hour trip to the Royal Children's Hospital.

We arrived in Brisbane with the ambulance siren sounding at 12.45pm. During the trip, I not only lost all movement in my body, but also lost my voice. I could no longer speak and I was in a state of total bewilderment. Everything had happened so fast that none of us knew what to think. Mum and Dad thought that I might actually die. They had never even heard of Guillain-Barré syndrome.

I was rushed into the Intensive Care Unit and placed on oxygen. They took a lumbar puncture to confirm the diagnosis and the next morning at 5.30 I was wheeled into theatre for a tracheotomy because I was struggling to breathe on my own. The last thing I remember is the lights of the theatre. Then everything went blank.

I have no memory of the first week after the tracheotomy. When I awoke I couldn't move — I could barely bat an eyelid. All I could do was lie on my back, staring at the ceiling, a pose that was not to change for the next four weeks. A respirator was breathing for me, tubes and drips entered and exited various parts of my body. My parents thought I was going to either die or be paralysed for life. I have to admit the same thought went through my mind on more than one occasion.

Days after the tracheotomy I was back in the operating theatre, this time to remove bladder stones!

Every day Mum sat by me as my condition got worse. 'He was all tubes and was just wasting away,' Mum remembers. 'The day after the tracheotomy he got very sick and the day after that his body got very weak. And he stayed like that for a few days. For those first few weeks we really didn't know which way he was going to go. We just hung in there,' Mum says.

I remember feeling very frustrated. I could hear everything and was aware of what was going on but I couldn't move to tell anyone. I would click my tongue to get the attention of a nurse, or to say 'yes'. To say 'no' I would close my eyes. That was how I communicated.

My parents feared that their fun-loving, active boy had gone forever. You can only imagine the emotions a parent experiences in those circumstances: their child paralysed, unable to move even a finger; the parent not knowing if their child will ever speak or walk again. And then, on St Patrick's Day, 11 days after I was rushed to hospital, there was the first flicker of movement in one of my fingers. It was a small sign. There was hope, and no one involved ever lost it. Every St. Patrick's day since, my sisters, my parents and I thank our lucky stars for this sign.

I had two younger sisters aged six and three and all they knew was that Kelvin was sick and Mum was away with him, and they were scared. They stayed on the farm with Dad, and it must have been incredibly hard on him. Like most men, Dad's not big on expressing emotion, but he must have been going through hell, wondering if his boy would ever recover.

The three of them would make the trip to Brisbane on weekends to see me but that's hardly an ideal situation for a young family. Young girls separated from their mother, not knowing what was happening to their brother and a father and husband in the same boat. It would have put Mum, Dad and the girls under tremendous strain and it is a credit to Mum's and Dad's strength of character and the bond between them that they didn't let it affect their marriage.

Mum stayed in Brisbane for the first seven weeks I was there. For the first week she stayed with her sister on the other side of town, catching two buses and travelling for an hour and a half every day, until hospital staff found her a room close to the Intensive Care Unit so she could be by my side at all times. Every day she would sit with me, massaging, stretching and exercising my fingers for hours at a time. That's a mother's love for you!

At lunch she would take a walk through the streets and parks of Brisbane, just to get away. She would catch a bus to Fortitude Valley and walk around the shops — anything for a bit of release from the emotional strain of watching her son lie there like a vegetable. Then she'd come back and sit by my side, working on my hands and talking to me, about anything and everything — what the weather was like and what my sisters were doing. Nearly every day Dr DeBuse would bring in around half a dozen student doctors to examine me; Guillain-Barré syndrome was so rare that it was an opportunity to educate that could not be missed.

The other kids in the ward were as young as 18 months and they were sick, very sick. So many died in the time I was there, according to Mum. My bed was in a corner of the ward, near the nurses' station so they could keep an eye on me. When someone got very sick, close to death, they would pull a screen around me so I didn't have to witness it. Mum and Dad could hear the awful sound of the flatline when someone didn't make it. I could hear it too.

I spent my ninth birthday in hospital. My family was there with balloons and a cake that I couldn't eat. The staff were wonderful, painting my face and singing 'Happy Birthday' to me. The whole time I was in hospital they would joke with me and keep my spirits up. Mum entered me in a competition in the *Sunday Sun*, and I won a soccer ball and had my photo in the paper. Lady Ramsay, wife of the then Queensland Governor Sir James, even paid me a visit.

After seven weeks, and no real signs of improvement, Mum returned home. Miss Marks, my physiotherapist who was also working on my muscles, could feel a slight difference in them, but it wasn't enough to enable any movement. Mum would travel between Kingaroy and Brisbane every weekend, and she and the doctors began to notice a gradual improvement in my condition.

While I was still in ICU I had developed kidney stones, which required two further operations, the second after they failed to find the stones the first time they opened me up. Then, to top it all off, when I was in the regular ward I contracted chicken pox. For every two steps forward there was one back.

Slowly but surely, over the weeks and months, I began to improve. After 13 weeks the doctors removed the tracheotomy, and just before I left intensive care, I spoke for the first time.

'Am I going to die?' I asked.

'No,' Mum said. 'You've come this far, there is no going back.'

Mum remembers: 'That's when he started fighting. He's a real fighter.'

I had no choice but to fight. The challenges just kept presenting themselves. After those first words it was just baby talk to begin with, and every bit of progress would be by baby steps. I had speech therapy and an occupational therapist who helped me learn to move my arms again, to hold things, to fasten buttons — which took a long, long time to master. I had lost the fine motor skills and my body needed to learn to perform them all over again. I couldn't feed myself and had to drink through a straw for a long time. Even when I graduated to drinking straight from the cup I needed someone to hold it for me.

After 16 weeks in intensive care I was able to sit up and be transferred in a wheelchair out of the ICU and into the Royal Children's Hospital. Dr Peter DeBuse was the doctor in charge of my care there, with a Dr Price visiting. I also had a special visit from a Professor Simpson, from Scotland, who was well-acquainted with the disease and told us it was now a case of waiting for the recovery and being prepared for a long, slow process.

Whilst I was initially a bit freaked out by the experience, I don't remember ever feeling depressed, or thinking 'woe is me'. As a kid, you just take what is thrown at you in life because you don't know anything else. It's frustrating because you want to be out and about, running around with your mates, but you accept the reality of your situation and try to make the best of it.

Mum remembers: 'He never once queried "why him?" He just accepted it and went with the flow. He was still the same cheeky Kelvin. But it was hard on him — very hard — as he needed help to get around. We used to take him out to Redcliffe to the seaside. There were no disabled toilets in those days so we'd have to take the bottle for him because he couldn't fit into the regular toilets.'

After a few months I was thrilled to be released home to the farm for two weeks, but that highlight was quickly tempered by the reality of the three-month hospital stint that followed. But it only made me more determined to recover, a characteristic that would drive me for the rest of my life.

Movement slowly returned, from my head to my toes, in the reverse order it had been taken from me. I had to learn to do everything again: sit up, move my arms, hold a fork — everything, from the most basic of movements.

I was lucky that the physiotherapist had stressed the importance of massaging and moving my hands while I was paralysed. They were clenched into fists but for hour after hour, every day, Mum would pry my fingers apart, stretch, straighten and massage them. When I did recover, my hands were the best part of my body and I have no doubt that's the reason I have made it as a bowler. The difference between my hands and feet is marked. Mum didn't work on my feet, and I still have circulation problems with them. She wonders 'what if' she had done the same with my feet as he did with my hands but nobody knew at the time how important or effective what she was doing would be. I certainly don't have anything but gratitude for the selfless dedication Mum displayed towards me for all those months. The patience and dedication of the doctors, nurses and, of course, Mum, is something for which I will forever be grateful.

For my physical therapy, Miss Marks would get into the hospital pool with me and move my legs every day. Then she moved on to my arms and got them going. I could only just sit up and was totally reliant on help to do so. Hospital staff would drum on my back for half an hour at a time to get all the phlegm out because it would fill my lungs and I didn't have the muscle capacity to cough it up myself. I would lie on my stomach and they would pound on my back. It felt like I was getting beaten up!

They would strap me to the bed for support and stand it up to put my weight on my feet. Slowly, day by day, I improved until I was eventually able to get around in a wheelchair, which was a real milestone.

We would set other milestones and the feeling of achieving one, as much as the actual effort that went into it, made me stronger and taught me my first lesson in goal-setting. Reaching milestones made me stronger. It felt like I was achieving something. I was reaching goals — and the feeling of getting better was encouragement to keep persevering. My muscles had totally wasted away and it took a lot of work to get them functioning again.

I had the use of my arms for a month before I could use my legs. Daily I would be up on the parallel bars, supporting my weight with my arms while trying to take some of the weight on my legs, and move them if I could. It was seven months into my recovery and I had splints on my feet to counter the foot drop. They went on every night and came off every morning. I went through it all, from the intense physio sessions in the hospital pool to the parallel bars, holding myself up with my arms and dragging my legs forward as I learnt to walk all over again. Slowly but surely, the signs of recovery were there, and Dr DeBuse told my parents they could expect me to make an almost complete recovery.

'It was a huge relief to know that in the end he would get

back to normal — pretty well,' Mum says. 'They could see that full movement in his feet wasn't going to come back, but otherwise he recovered pretty much back to normal. It filled us with happiness and hope that he would have a normal life. But it wasn't until a couple of years later when he started walking again, without the callipers, that we were truly convinced of his recovery.'

I entered hospital in March 1978 and left in September. When I finally went home for good, it was in a modified chair equipped with wheels. Not a wheelchair, but an ordinary chair altered to help me get around. It was lowered and I would lie on my stomach across the cushion and use my arms to pull myself around.

Did I mention my recovery was slow? I was on my tummy on that chair for close to a year, sleeping with those hard plastic splints wrapped in cotton wool strapped to my arms and legs, from my hands to my elbows and my ankles to my knees. The hospital also made me special shoes to counteract my footdrop.

Once I was able to start walking, the doctors applied the callipers to support my still-weak legs. They were horrible metallic things that buckled around my ankles, calves and just below my knees. They were very uncomfortable and I hated them. I would push our old lawn mower around the dirt road leading from the main road past our house and around the garage. At first I couldn't walk more than 10 or 20 metres but as I got stronger I was able to walk further. I hated those callipers, but they were a great motivating factor for me to get out there and push that lawn mower. It was with great relish after three months that I threw the damn things away for good. Walking was still an effort but that just made me try harder. I always had the attitude that 'I can do it'.

When I went back to school, I had to negotiate about 20 steps, which I would do by sitting on my bottom and using my arms to raise myself up each step. I was still in my custom-made wheelchair at this stage. Picking me up from home, the bus driver would get out and put my chair in the bus, carrying me to my seat. Once at school, my chair would stay outside at the foot of the steps. My sister would do the potty run, emptying the potty whenever I had to go at school so I didn't have to go back down those stairs again. I was determined to get up the steps on my own, but other kids would help me back down

The kids in Wooroolin were great to me. I copped a bit of teasing once we moved to the Gold Coast and went to high school, but when the kids saw that I was trying to be the same as everyone else, they were all really encouraging. I would try to run but I would fall over, no doubt providing amusement for anyone watching. But I never got mad, just occasionally disappointed. I would get up and go again; what else was I going to do?

I did not regain the use of the tendons required to lift my feet, meaning my feet just hung limply from my ankles. That's why I needed the special shoes, to stabilise my feet and ensure they didn't drag behind me as I walked.

It took two years before I fully recovered, except for the foot drop. That's a long time, but as I've said, as a kid you just accept your fate and get on with it. Life is a series of cause and effect and you react to the circumstances in which you find yourself. I would probably never have taken up lawn bowls

— certainly not at such a young age — if I had not contracted Guillain-Barré syndrome. I might not ever have developed the determination and persistence required to excel at the level I did if I had not learned to set goals and never give up. Life's funny like that. It's like the old saying: *If life gives you lemons, make lemonade.* I reckon I could teach Schweppes a thing or two.

3

First Steps

The first time I ever rolled a bowl I was sitting in a wheelchair. It was a hot day, just before my twelfth birthday. Dad stood on the back green at Wondai, picked me up in my chair and lifted me off the bank onto the green beside him. I wouldn't call it a mystical experience or say I fell in love with the game at first sight but I loved being on that grass. Just to be outside and doing something — anything — was a thrill. I didn't care what it was; it just happened to be bowls.

Dad lined me up and Mum stood about ten metres in front of me on the green. I dropped my right arm to my side and Dad placed a bowl in my hand. It was heavy and hard to grip. Despite all the work Mum had done on my fingers, they still lacked strength and it was all I could do to hold onto it, let alone roll it any real distance. My first attempt died before it reached Mum and my second was no better. My first bowling experience consisted of two ends before I was exhausted, but it was a start. I could do something.

That first month I had another two or three attempts. Week by week my strength returned, giving me a better grip and more control. The muscles in my arms adapted and my length increased. After about six months of bowling, two years after I left hospital, I faced a new challenge. I was going to learn to walk again.

The road to recovery had begun back in the Royal Children's Hospital in Brisbane, with the twice-daily physio sessions in the hydrotherapy pool. For months into my recovery I suffered intense 'pins and needles' in my legs, feet, toes and hands because of poor circulation. The physios would work my muscles, running their thumbs down my calves to get the blood flowing back to areas it had barely visited for months. They worked me hard and it was painful. Every time I have had a massage since, I wince at the memory.

The pool sessions relieved the pins and needles. They strapped floaties to my arms, sat me in a hydraulic chair and lowered me into the stainless steel hydrotherapy pool. The 32-degree water warmed my muscles and the buoyancy supported them, allowing me to independently move my legs for the first time.

It was a buzz being out of the wheelchair but it was hard work. My crutches were the kind with the hoops at the forearm and elbow rather than the ones that go under your armpits, and I remember my arms burning from taking the load my legs couldn't bear. My upper body gained strength pretty quickly but my legs took much longer. In all it was a three-year process learning to walk again, but there was no way I was ever going to do anything else. That was my attitude and that of those around me. It was just a question of taking the steps, so to speak.

The hospital fitted me for callipers, which they bolted

into the back of my shoes. My feet were locked in the flexed position, which helped me with balance and walking because they couldn't dangle down off the ankle. It meant I didn't have to lift my feet as high when walking, which was just as well as I had steel bars buckled to my legs up to the knee. As much as I loved being out of the chair, I hated those callipers. The doctors told me to wear them so I wore them and used them in conjunction with the crutches; however, I took them off as often as I could.

When bowling I would support my weight with my left arm and crutch as I took the right crutch away. My legs were weak and wobbly at the knees and with foot drop in both feet it was hard just keeping my balance. Getting down low and remaining still at the point of delivery was a challenge, and it was also an effort getting from end to end. I was worn out after 20 minutes but I kept at it.

After a month I was able to discard the crutches, but for two bloody years I wore those callipers from when I got out of bed in the morning to when I got back in at night. When I went back to school in grade eight I wore them under my tracksuit pants. Of course, as a 13-year-old, I was self-conscious and didn't want to wear them, but Mum and Dad forced me to and I'm glad they did. As my legs got stronger and more used to bearing my weight, I would avoid putting them on each morning for as long as I could. I would have breakfast, then sit in front of the TV, play with the dog — anything to delay the inevitable order from Mum or Dad to get them on.

I remember when I first stood without the aid of crutches, on the timber floor of our main lounge room. I discarded the crutches and stood there for about 20 or 30 seconds before I crumpled to the floor. I think Mum was in the kitchen because I vaguely remember her coming in and asking me what the hell I was doing.

My legs were too heavy to move initially but that improved very quickly once I could stand. The strength in my legs came back quickly and I was up and away. I probably looked awkward to everyone else but I was flying. As soon as I could I threw away the callipers, which the hospital replaced with plastic insert 'splints' that fitted into my shoes and ran up the back of my legs, correcting the foot drop for as long as I wore them.

I was there on the back green every Sunday afternoon for a year I reckon, chipping away. Mum and Dad would play on the front green, the girls would play with their dolls, and I would sit behind the bank of the main green and watch all the bowlers until I got bored and had a roll myself out the back. Throw in a Sarsaparilla and chips and a wade through the creek bed on the golf course collecting balls, and it was a good family day out. Walking the one-kilometre length of that creek bed was great exercise as well as a nice little earner. Walking around our dirt track with the lawn mower at this time also began to wean me off the crutches.

As for the game, as much as it was a therapeutic activity and 'something I could do', it was also something I strove to be good at and over time my stamina, balance, skill, knowledge and enjoyment of the sport grew.

I started with a set of old bowls borrowed from the clubhouse but after a while my parents bought me my first set of Henselite Super Grip bowls, size zero. It was an old set, but that didn't matter to me. They had a picture of a heron on them — the same image that years later would appear on the trophy plate for the Gold Coast Winter Carnival. I still have those bowls and the plate is hanging on my wall, so maybe it was fate.

When I was 14 my parents sold the farm and we moved to Elanora on the Gold Coast. It was an adjustment moving from a small country town and I initially copped a bit from some of the kids at Palm Beach High, but that's teenagers I guess. I never let it bother me.

We joined the Currumbin RSL and with about a year of bowling behind me, I could feel I was getting better. I could now ride my bike the kilometre or so to and from school, pack my bowls onto my bike rack and ride the kilometre and a half to the RSL for an after-school roll-up, which I would do maybe three or four times a week. I was getting keen.

There was no junior competition back then so I would wait for the club bowlers to finish and go inside for a drink, and then I had the green to myself. At first I practiced only short ends because it was easier for me.

I grew the confidence to enter the Brunswick Heads schoolboy singles (18 and under) in1983 when I was only 14, although I was really only making up the numbers. At the time there were only about 20 junior bowlers in the region, but the experience of playing against these bowlers, that included the likes of Cameron Curtis made me feel as though I was part of something and not just a kid who had taken up bowls because he couldn't do anything else. It gave me the incentive to practice and then practice some more so that I would be competitive the next time round. The following year my parents drove me to the Brunswick Heads club and I remember the nerves kicking in when I first stepped onto the green. While I still had doubts about my ability, I was feeling more confident than the year before. My parents, who were my number one supporters were just happy to see me out on the paddock and being able to participate. I think I surprised myself and my parents when I won the competition that year. My mother definitely had a tear in her eye. It was the first time that I really believed there may be a future for me in the game.

My game improved to the stage that I entered the 1984 Queensland junior championships. I was 15 and there wasn't a lot of competition in those days, but I lost in the first round anyway. Nevertheless, the taste of competition spurred me on. I had just beaten Phil Mallett, a leading singles player who had a lot more experience than me, to win the Gold Coast Colts' under-45-years-old 'pewter' competition and was playing in my father's team, which was joint leader in the Surfer's Paradise Superbowl competition, when bowls and life were put on an abrupt hold by another operation.

The specialists told me they thought they could fix my foot drop by fusing my ankle. They told me it would give me a better-than-even chance of improvement, so I said okay, let's go for it, and the decision was made to fuse my right ankle. The surgeon cut open my foot in a wide arc from the outside near the heel. They inserted a pin in my big toe, running up through the centre of my foot, broke my ankle and stapled the bones together. For six weeks my leg was encased in plaster to the thigh and the ankle itself was in plaster for three months. I then wore an ankle brace and had to practically learn to walk all over again.

My toes swelled like balloons and the pain was immense, indescribable, like having a knife stuck in me. I had to keep my foot up and it set me back a long way — I didn't bowl for about six months. I still suffer arthritis in my right ankle. There was no way I was going to go through that with the left foot. I'd rather have the foot drop! I've got a bit of an awkward limp to this day, but I manage and I'm in less pain than if they'd fused my left ankle too.

As I recovered from the ankle fusion I eased back into bowling and, much to my delight, found that my improvement continued. The hospital gave me a walking stick to maintain my balance at the point of delivery and it worked so well that I still use it.

I announced my come-back by finishing runner-up to Steve Glasson in the 1985 Queensland junior championships at Pine Rivers. The following year in the 1986 championships I beat Jeff Hall from Mount Isa East 25–15 in the first round, and in the semis I beat Tim Padovan 25–13. I then went on to win the final 25–14 against Mark Parella (Rob's son) to clinch my first state junior singles title.

When I was 18 I became eligible to play in the club championships and won the pairs with Dad. It was the first club pairs title I'd ever won. To top it off, I also won the singles the same year. I enjoyed the winning feeling and these victories gave me the self-belief that would propel me into the next stage of my career.

Dad was a very good competitive club bowler, and one of the better bowlers at the Currumbin Bowls Club. We had been through so much together with my illness, and Dad had always been there to encourage me. So to win my first ever pairs competition with Dad was fitting, and a thrill for both of us. It was one of those rare moments that I'll always cherish.

Good Influences

Robbie Dobbins encouraged me to move from Currumbin RSL to the Coolangatta Bowls Club as he wanted to take me under his wing and have me play with him in the district pairs and fours. He also believed that playing with top-class bowlers at Coolangatta would improve my game.

Robbie was absolutely right. Playing with him in the District Pairs taught me how to read a head and to determine the correct shot to play. As well as receiving the benefit of Robbie's coaching, once at Coolangatta, I also came under the influence of Ian Schuback, a current Australian player at that time, and Bob Purcell, a long-time state player.

I was a bit nervous training with Bob Purcell at first as he was a real legend of the sport and was known as a great coach. He would have been in his 60s then. He fine-tuned my technique by straightening me out and getting rid of bad habits. He taught me to point both feet and shoulders in the direction of the intended trajectory of the bowl and to stay down and follow through after the point of delivery rather than coming up too quickly. He had a real long-term effect on my career.

He taught me long ends, encouraging me to 'play ditch to ditch'. 'Roll the jack and play to the jack,' he'd say. Up until then my strength had been in short ends, but Bob worked with me, ensuring I got my balance right at the point of delivery. I used to take a big step into my delivery but Bob made me shorten it, which helped make me more balanced and enabled me to be more consistent on long ends.

Every Saturday morning for six months Bob would stand at one end of the green and I would be at the other, rolling the bowls to him. If he didn't like a particular effort, he would pick up the bowl and hurl it back down to me and make me do it again. 'You crossed the line,' he'd yell. Or, 'You're under the line,' and I would try again.

Bob was a tall, skinny and tough bloke. I remember having to look up at him all the time. I looked up at him and I looked up to him. If he said something, he meant it and if you did something wrong you'd have to do it again.

Thanks to Bob I learned to adapt my game so that if I was getting beaten I could change the game up, such as change the length of ends. He gave me a lot of tips, like playing one side of the green. 'Pick the kindest side of the green,' he'd say, which most of the time would be the wider hand. He'd tell me to do something and explain why I should do it. 'Let the wind work for you rather than fight against it,' he told me.

In my early years of bowling I used to take my green by just imagining the arc. No one had told me any different. Then Bob told me to imagine a line between the mat and the jack, and pick a point on the bank such as a chair leg, a peg or a scoreboard. While I used this method for a while, I decided what worked better for me was to focus on the point in the green where the bowl would start to turn in its arc towards the kitty. This became more natural to me than trying to adjust to a new mark on the bank when the length of end changed.

I'm so grateful to Bob for opening my eyes to the possibilities in the game. He taught me most of what I know about bowls, and he toughened me up!

After Bob had coached me for a year, Rob Parella took me under his wing and changed my game again. He was an Australian singles player at that time, so I was thrilled and surprised when he asked me to play in the Gold Coast Winter Fours as his third. He saw me as an up-and-coming player. This was a real highlight of my young career.

Rob was an aggressive type of player. I learned to drive just by watching him. He was the best driver the game's ever seen. Driving is like hitting a golf ball off the tee; if you try too hard you'll pull it to the left or spoon it to the right, and Rob made it look so easy. He showed me how to stand on the mat and how to hold the bowl for a drive, to spread the fingers a bit more. 'None of this pussy weight; just hit it,' he'd tell me. I got my speed from him and became one of the fastest drivers in the game.

Rob was also a flamboyant player, more youthful than most bowls players at that time — although as a man in his 40s he was a lot older than his three playing partners in that first winter carnival. He was an innovator who was instrumental in changing the way bowls is played and definitely one of the greatest characters to ever play the game.

It was a great experience to play with Rob in the Winter

Carnival and I learnt a new aspect to the game. The drive helped my game a lot. Rob is Italian and he used to play bocce, so he had an eye like a hawk. He was short, stocky and very strong. He had the perfect build to drive hard and he probably drove twice as much as anyone else. No one could get a shot on him. He had the killer instinct and drove people off the paddock. I was probably too nice but he was there to win, and he didn't mind a bit of gamesmanship. He would get in his opponent's line and talk to his bowl as he followed it up the green, always in his opponent's line of sight. He would do things like finish an end and disappear into the clubhouse for five minutes.

Rob would say, 'Don't talk to the opposition,' and he would slow the game down to annoy them. I have employed some of these tactics myself at times. I've deliberately slowed the game up, 'gone to the toilet' for a few minutes, that sort of thing. When you're behind you've got to change the momentum somehow by trying something different.

Rob mentally toughened me up. He always told me: 'We're gunna beat these bastards no matter what. Don't worry about them; just concentrate on what we're doing. We're here to win.'

The 1988 Gold Coast Winter Carnival was held in the third week of July, culminating in the final on the Friday. We had five games in our section and won all of them.

We then went into the knockout phase, where the last 16 were whittled down to the final two: us and the Tweed Heads team of Stan Coomber, Albert Dawson, Artie Booth and Freddie Lewis, who were all mainstays of Queensland bowling — veterans, especially compared with us teenagers. Freddie would have been old enough to be our grandfather!

The final was my first experience in front of a large crowd. People were massed five deep around the green at Tweed Heads Bowling Club and there were TV cameras trained on us. For us young blokes it was like nothing we'd ever experienced before. The fact that our opponents were on their home rink added to the pressure and the sense that we were underdogs.

The match began at 9.30am, with the greens at around 14 seconds. They would speed up as the game went on. It was a close game and we got off to a nervous start. We had three kids at one end and Rob Parella at the other and soon enough we were down 8–3.

As the game went on we started to relax and play better as a team. Rob was pretty tough on the first two and got stuck into us all, telling us, 'I can't win this on my own.' He was a fighter — he never conceded defeat until the last bowl was rolled. Mid-match he got us all together in the middle of the green for a pep talk. 'Give me some bowls at the start,' he said.

Rob played an awesome match. We gave him some help but he backed us up to the hilt. The match lasted four hours, and with Rob's devastating drive killing several ends, the allotted 21 ends stretched out to 26. I remember playing a telling shot on about the 18th end when Rob asked me to drive the jack into the ditch, and all his tuition paid off when the jack and bowl thudded into the sand.

The 3000 strong crowd was on our side. They cheered loudly every time we got within a couple of feet of the jack, while our opponents could have a toucher and all they'd get was a polite clap.

We were ten shots up with four ends to play, but the 'oldies' used all their experience to get back to within striking distance. With one end to play, they needed four shots to tie and five to win. With his last bowl, the 74-year-old Lewis fell in for three shots and, after the marathon four-and-a-half-hour match, we won by one! The final result of 21–20 made our team, dubbed the 'teen machine', the youngest in history to win a major event in lawn bowls.

Speaking at the presentation of the prize-money immediately after the match, Rob praised each member of the team and I was bursting with pride when he made a special mention of me, saying: 'I call him my backstop. Every time we were in trouble, he was there. He drew, he drove and he drew to the ditch.'

To top it off, the tournament organisers described the match as 'the best thing to happen to bowls in the last ten years'. I'm still wondering what happened ten years before that could have been better! I really think that this victory and the media attention it created paved the way for bowls to be seen as not only the domain of the elderly, but also a mainstream sport for younger people.

After we won, the 14-year-old Vardy, who had to take a week off school to play, was interviewed on TV and asked what he was going to do with his $1500 prize money, to which he replied, 'I'm going to buy some lollies!'

Pocket Money

To earn a bit of extra cash, I started mowing a few lawns around my local Currumbin/Palm Beach area. To drum up business I produced some fliers, got on my pushbike and did a letterbox drop. Before long I had quite a few regular clients whose lawns I would mow once every couple of weeks in winter, and once a week in summer when the grass grew more quickly. It worked well because I could earn enough to enter bowls tournaments that usually ran from Monday to Thursday, and I would take care of most of my lawns on a Friday and some on Saturday mornings before pennant. Many of the clients became my good friends who followed my bowling career and were understanding if I let their lawns grow a bit longer if I was playing in a tournament. To this day, my father still mows the lawns for five or six of those original clients from 20 years ago to keep active and supplement his pension.

I was always looking at ways to make a few extra dollars and my greatest passion besides playing bowls was beach fishing. As anyone who also enjoys this kind of fishing knows, the best bait, especially for whiting, are beach worms. The problem is that worms are really difficult to catch and I spent hours trying to catch the little buggers. They pop their heads out of the sand and they're super quick to slip back out of sight. After school I would go to the beach for a couple of hours just to try and catch one of these worms. I didn't have much success. Then, one afternoon, I met a gentleman on the beach who showed me the knack of catching a worm. He said, 'When they pop their heads out and they arch their backs, their feelers relax and you just grab 'em.' I got one straight away after he showed me, and from then on I got better and better at it.

So I applied to the Department of Primary Industries for a beach worming licence, which was required if you wanted to catch more than about 20 worms. Back then it cost me $100 to apply for the licence, but I soon paid that off by selling the worms for 20 cents each, which over time went up to 80 cents. It wasn't bad money when I was catching between 150 and 200 worms in a couple of hours, and I enjoyed going to the beach. I would put some fish remains in an onion-sack and swirl it in the shallows up and down the beach on a length of rope. The smell of the fish attracts the beach worms so they would pop their heads up about a half inch and I could see a little V-shaped bump when the wave washed back as a sign of where they were and I would then scoop them up.

I did this for six or seven years, and it was a good earner over Christmas, Easter and summer weekends. Part of the condition of getting the beach worm licence was that I send in a quarterly report to the Department of Primary Industry detailing how many worms I had caught, and when my bowls career started to take off and I no longer had time for worming, the reports started to show nil activity. The result was that I lost my beach worming permit, which is a shame as they are now worth about $30,000! I still enjoy going down to the beach at sunset with the family and catching a few worms.

So I was pretty busy with my lawn mowing and catching beach worms on Thursday afternoons to sell to the bait shop for the weekend trade. On top of this, I also had a night-time job as a 'glassie' at the local live band venue, but I'll tell you about that a little later.

6

Playing for Queensland

The victory in the Winter Carnival gave me the confidence I needed to take my game to the next level.

In 1989 I won the Gold Coast Winter Carnival singles and pairs, which were major events back then, and the same year I was victorious in the club singles and triples at Coolangatta in my first year as a member. My coach, Bob Purcell, won the pairs. In the triples my teammates were Rusty Newton, who played lead, and Neil Crichton, who skipped.

I also made my debut for Queensland in the national sides championships in Enoggera, Brisbane, in 1989. I received a letter in the mail from the Queensland Bowls chairman of selectors, Stuart Keys, to notify me of my selection, and to this day we are still notified by mail. It was a bit of a shock at the time as no one as young as me had ever been selected to play for the state side. I was still only 19 and working at Tweed City Kmart. My goals had changed as my career began to take off; I had set my sights on one day representing my state, maybe in my early 20s, but I didn't expect it to come so soon. A lot of players then were in the 40–55 age group. Now the average age is more like 25 and if you're over 40 you're a senior player. Steve Glasson came into the Queensland team a year after me, and Cam Curtis debuted for NSW around the same time.

I really appreciated the support of my teammates at Coolangatta who passed around the hat to raise money for the purchase of my first Queensland maroon state blazer that they presented to me for my 19th birthday.

The top 16 players from each state were divided into four teams of four. I played with Ken Williams, Col Pritchard and Trevor Morris, who was the Australian skip at the time. There was a bit of pressure and I was nervous, but I had been playing well leading up to the tournament.

My Queensland debut was a three test series against Western Australia at Sandgate Bowls Club in Brisbane. In the first game I was uptight and shaky for the first half but my teammates were fantastic. They were all very experienced and made me feel at home, which helped me to settle in. It was the best time I could have dreamt of to debut for my state, with two Australian representatives and Col as Queensland champion. After the nerves were out of the way I relaxed and played pretty well on debut.

The match came down to the last game of the tournament and at about the halfway mark, Queensland was 50 shots behind. In one telling end, my rink had the best seven bowls behind the head and Col Pritchard called Trevor Morris for a trail of the kitty. Trevor nonchalantly obliged, trailing the jack for seven shots. That lifted the other rinks and going into the last end Queensland had levelled the scores 88–88 and came home and won by three shots overall. Our rink was a formidable team and won six out of its seven games. We ended up winning the series 2–1, and followed this with another test series against South Australia at Newmarket Bowls Club the next day, which we also won 2–1. This led into the National Sides Championships which was then called the Alley Shield, the 'bees knees' of state bowls where we played a round robin against all other states and territories at Inogera Bowls Club. We were victorious again, completing a 'clean sweep' for Queensland and a dream debut for myself.

An obstacle I had to overcome in this tournament was that I was playing while on antibiotics, which my doctor had prescribed to help curb the pain from an infected toenail on my left foot that couldn't be removed because of excessive swelling. To make matters worse, two weeks before, two bones in my right foot had been cracked during an accident on the Gold Coast. I was out having a drink with some friends and when we got out of the cab, the driver ran over my foot. One of my mates yelled out to him and he reversed back to see what was wrong and ran over it again! So, I did have my problems, but rather than dwell on them or look for sympathy, I used them to spur myself on.

Ken Williams was the best 'second' in Australia at that time. He was a current Australian player and a great guy to have playing after me if I didn't get near the head. He was down-to-earth and nothing worried him. No matter if we were behind or in front, he would show the same body language. He was cool and rock solid. He would pick up my bowl, polish it, give it to me before I'd bowl and say, 'Relax, do your natural thing.' He was a member of South Tweed and one of the older guys then, about 55. He was tall, thin and liked a cigarette. He was fit-looking but tragically died of cancer. He was missed big-time when he passed away.

Col Pritchard was from the Sunshine Coast. He was a new-and-used car salesman who would have been in his late 40s then and was a solid guy who liked a beer. He never played for Australia but played frequently for Queensland. He was the state singles champ around that time and was a real in-form player through the late 80s. He was a real nice sociable guy who was very supportive, great to play with and could knock down six to eight schooners after a game. I enjoyed his company, but I drank Coke most of the time. Although at the end of the round-robin section (four days) Col and Kenny relaxed with a drink so I joined in. I guess they 'christened' me during that session!

Trevor Morris was a pretty cool dude from Cairns. He was tall, trim, about 40, with a black moustache. He drank rum and Coke, never beer. He was calm and collected with a ton of natural ability and showed no nerves. In fours, the format is two bowls each, and Trevor was known for being one of the best with two bowls, so he was good to have playing the last two. Trevor let his bowls do the talking and was always very supportive, clapping your bowl if it was good or not so good.
Before I'd go out to play he'd say, 'Kelvin, just relax. We've got a great team, don't worry about anything. Just be relaxed. The more relaxed you are the better you'll play.' I took that on over the years because it's true and I'd say the same thing to any bowler now.

With the confidence and experience I gained from playing at the state level I was starting to play consistently really well.

The first round of the 1989 Coolangatta Club Championships was played in October with the following rounds spaced out over the months ahead. I beat David Wills 25–10 in the final to become, at 20 years of age, the youngest player in the club's 40-year history to win the club singles. To win this event at a strong club — and there were a lot of good district bowlers there — was a personal achievement that I rate highly.

The following year (1990), I was again selected in the Queensland side that played in the State Sides Championships in Sandy Bay, Tasmania. However, we won only four of seven games, and to be perfectly honest, I was partly to blame.

I probably stepped over the line with alcohol consumption. I was 20 and only weighed about 65–70kg, so I'd have five or six beers and become Franz Liszt!

To make matters worse, it was my first interstate trip and I probably didn't play as well as I could. The greens in Tasmania were slower than I was accustomed to and I had never played on Bent grass before. It's slower and turns more and I struggled to find the right weight and line.

I was dropped from the next team picked for Queensland. I was not told why I was dropped, but apart from not playing as well as I could, the selectors certainly didn't like my drinking and playing up. It was a learning curve for me.

After returning home I regained good form and continued winning events, so my name was still in front of the selectors.

Up and Away

I was invited to play in the Hub of the Hunter championship at the East Maitland Bowling Club in Newcastle. I invested in a bus ticket and travelled south for the tournament. The organisers gave me $100 to cover my expenses for the five days, and I stayed in the local caravan park so that I could have a bit left over to eat! I certainly appreciated the invitation to play at the event and the financial contribution, but it was insignificant compared to the money spent to bring Clive Lanahan from South Africa to compete. John Snell made relatively easy work of beating Lanahan 31–13 on his way to the final, while I took five and a half hours to overcome the NSW champion, Bob King, 31–28. I then went on to beat Snell 31–19 to take the title and the much-needed winner's cheque of $3,000. I was two days shy of my 23rd birthday and couldn't have asked for a better present.

This win in a major tournament was a breakthrough for my career, and the following media release was sent out from the tournament committee:

BRILLIANT PERFORMANCE BY KERKOW WINS

'HUB OF THE HUNTER TITLE'

The first major win of 22-year-old Queenslander Kelvin Kerkow's bowls career came at East Maitland Bowling Club in the annual Hub of the Hunter singles bowls tournament this afternoon.

Basically unknown outside his state, Kelvin was the only player in the field of top internationals, Australian and state representatives to win all his games.

His wins from games, section and first prize saw this young man, considered by many as a future Australian representative, totalled about $3000.

Kerkow started his game against John Snell of Lake Cathie on a 17-second green with signs of a few nerves, but by the 12th end led 8–7.

He increased his lead to ten shots before Snell won back the mat on end 19; however, the youngster with an old head on young shoulders held out the tough international to win by 12 shots.

END

Terry McHugh, Secretary of the 1992 Hub of the Hunter Bowls Committee

My next major event was a month later when I played in the ANZ District Pairs and Fours Championship at Burleigh Heads. Robbie Dobbins and I managed to make it through a field of about 120 teams to the pairs final, where we came up against Clarrie Watkins and Ken Riddle of South Tweed Heads.

On the 13th end of the final we were trailing 9–15 and holding four shots when Ken picked up the shot with a wick bowl that rested just in front of the kitty. Robbie and I decided that there was only a slim chance of removing the bowl if I played a little over draw weight, so a full-blooded drive was the only real option. I drove with my first and took out the shot bowl, and when Ken's second bowl didn't change things, Robbie called out to me, 'Now play the perfect shot!' He had always given me good advice, so I obliged with a resting toucher, picking up five shots and bringing the score to 14–15. We picked up another three shots on the 19th end and went into the last three shots up. I put the match beyond doubt by trailing the kitty with my last to pick up the shot and the title.

Mum and Dad (Joan and Ivan), were and still are my biggest fans. They were working as volunteers on crowd control and scoreboards at the event, but a family wedding in Gladstone took them away for 36 hours, including while the final was being played. Dad phoned the Burleigh Heads Club just before the wedding to hear that Robbie and I were in the lead, and as soon as the married couple had exchanged vows he was on the phone again to get the news of our victory. I hear that he really let the confetti fly outside the church!

Robbie and I then backed up in the fours with our Coolangatta team-mates, Kim Weaver and Bob Moir. Robbie had groomed me to take over as skip, and this was to be my trial by fire. We jumped to a 5–2 lead after five ends and there was no stopping us after that. Even though I was skipping, Robbie had great influence from third position, giving encouragement to the team, playing some extraordinary shots and giving me perfect direction. We advanced to 16–4 after 13 ends and, much to our delight, the game was called off when we were 24–11 up on the 20th end.

The cheques I received for both of these wins were much needed. I was becoming increasingly dependent on winnings from tournaments to help pay the bills and allow me to take the time to devote to the game I love.

I managed to get back into the next State Championships Team the following year, a little bit older and a lot wiser.

In 1993 I was picked for the Australian under-25 squad. Five up-and-coming players went to Hong Kong to play against the Hong Kong under 25s. The other team members were Steve Glasson, Adam Gleeson, Peter Harris and Adam Jeffrey, with Robbie Dobbins as coach and Keith Poole as manager. A few months earlier, Bowls Australia had told me to get a passport because the trip was coming up and I was selected in an initial squad of 14.

It was my first international trip, and Hong Kong blew me away. We stayed in Nathan Road and all I remember is the continuous stream of cars going past. Walking out of the foyer, I'd never seen the likes of the traffic and masses of people, the smell of food being cooked on the footpath, the people eating on the footpath … It was a real eye-opener. We visited the markets at night, which were still kicking at 10pm, and bought some watches, although I didn't have a lot of money and couldn't get my head around the exchange rate.

We played at the Kowloon Cricket Club and played well, losing the first day but winning the next two. It was a great experience for me as I had never seen bowling greens so rough and bumpy ever before in my bowls career.

On 28 June 1993 the Coolangatta Bowls Club hosted the 21st Anniversary Master of Masters. The twelve most highly qualified singles players in Australia are invited to play at this event, and I was pleased to accept my invitation. The field was divided into Section A and Section B. Section A consisted of Katunarich (WA), Snell (NSW), Schuback (Qld), Anderson (Qld), Curtis (NSW), and Parrella (Qld). Section B comprised Taylor (SA), Sutcliffe (Vic), Kerkow (Qld), Ball (WA), Steinhardt (Qld), and Dalton (Vic).

Anyone who knows their bowls will agree that there was a bit of talent amongst that lot! Not only were bragging rights at stake, but also a winner's cheque of $3,000 (which was a fair bit of coin back then) and a holiday for two to Argentina courtesy of Aerolineas Argentinas, one of the tournament's major sponsors.

I finished the sectional play with four wins, including a nine-shot victory over Geoff Sutcliffe, who was the current Australian singles champion. I lost my fourth round match against Denis Dalton 25–23, the same player who had kept me out of the final of my first invitation to this event the previous year. However, the defeat was not enough to keep me out of the final this time, and I was up against the winner of Section A, none other than one of my great mentors, Rob Parrella.

It is interesting to look back at how each of us was profiled in the event's programme, and it will give you an idea of the track record of the man I was up against and where I was at in my career:

ROB PARELLA- KEDRON QLD. International and state

representative. One of the world's best with impressive 60 Masters Championships and International titles. 1992 wins include State Singles, Jack High Singles, Adelaide Masters Singles and State Fours.

KELVIN KERKOW – COOLANDATTA QLD. State Representative and A.I.S. squad member. Within one shot of playing in last year's final at his first attempt. 1992 was big year winning District Pairs and Fours, Winter Carnival Mayoral Trophy being runner-up Singles and Fours, Merrilands Masters Pairs, Hub of Hunter Masters Singles, Club Pairs and Triples, Grafton Masters Fours.

Rob was a previous three-time winner of the event and after a tight score-line of 9–8 to Rob after nine ends, most of the spectators assumed he was on his way to a fourth title when he held me scoreless for half an hour to go 21–9 up. I just couldn't get my weight right on the narrow hand in the breezy conditions, but then I thought to myself, 'What the hell, why not give the wide hand a try?' This tactic paid off and I started to get back into the match, chasing my bowls to the head. The crowd swung its support behind me. I kept Rob scoreless for the next hour and pegged his lead back to level the scores at 23-all on the 36th end with a forehand up-shot that trailed the jack into the ditch. Then, on the 37th end, I held game shots on three occasions, each time Rob killing the end with his trademark 'bullet' drive. With his fourth drive, to the astonishment of the crowd, and no doubt Rob, he took out his own bowl to go down by two shots.

I rate this as my biggest comeback to win a tournament.

It almost seemed like a miracle, and what made it all the more memorable was that it was against the great man. Rob was philosophical about losing, saying: 'When you're in a tournament like this, someone up there has already decided who's going to win it, and today wasn't my day.'

One of the rewards of winning the Master of Masters was the trip to South America, so my fiancée, Karen, and I packed our bags and jetted off in business class via Sydney and New Zealand to Rio de Janeiro in Brazil. It was our first overseas trip together and we were in for a bit of culture shock. We had our own tour guide who met us at the airport with our name on a sign and he could speak English. When we got to the hotel, the staff could speak English as well. But when we went down the street at our first opportunity, after we'd exchanged money, no one could speak a word of English. It's not that I really expected them to — after all, it's their country and their language — but when we went to McDonald's I tried to order a Big Mac value meal and they didn't have a clue what I was talking about. I ended up having to point. I couldn't even order a Coke for Karen without being given lemonade. So it was really weird and we wondered how long we were going to be able to cope.

Once we got over our culture shock Rio was fantastic and we had a great time. We spent a couple of days relaxing on the beach in warm sunshine. The beach was a couple hundred metres wide — it was just like the Gold Coast except that every patch of sand was occupied and there were many more bikini-clad bodies.

One of the highlights of the trip was visiting the Iguazu Waterfalls. To this day, it is probably the most awesome thing

I've ever seen. Apparently Niagara Falls is the tallest, but Iguazu is the widest waterfall in the world. We stayed in a hotel overlooking the falls, and the sight and the thunderous noise was unbelievable. We travelled on a big rubber boat upstream through rapids and then drove through the jungle in a Land Rover, with monkeys swinging through the trees and big orange toucan birds flying overhead.

⊙ ⊙ ⊙

After winning the Queensland state pairs in May 1994 with Andrew Waddell and the Rum City Singles in Bundaberg in July, I set myself for the Golden Nugget Invitation Prestige Singles in August. Since it first started in 1986, The Golden Nugget has become the most prestigious singles event in Australia. Each year the best twelve players in Australia are invited to play by the Tweed Heads Bowls Club, so it's the best of the best and there are no easy games. Every year it attracts a crowd of thousands and is probably the best attended bowls event in Australia. A lot of Victorians migrate north for the winter to play some bowls and watch the event.

I was thrilled to have been invited to play as it was recognition of being the reigning Coolangatta Master of Masters singles champion and Gold Coast – Tweed champion of club champions in both pairs and singles. In the Golden Nugget I was in the esteemed company of players such as Steve Anderson, who was just back from skipping the Australian men's triples and fours teams to gold medals at the Pacific Championships in Canada; my Masters' final opponent Rob

Parella; Victorian singles champion Mark Jacobsen; and defending Nugget champion Ian Schuback, to name just a few.

I did pretty well in my section by accounting for four Australian representatives on my way to the final against Steve Anderson. It was an epic final lasting two and half hours with a thriller ending. After being tied 8–8, I opened up a 23–12 lead before Steve fought back to 24–17 going into what was to be the final end. I was holding shot when Steve moved the kitty back towards the ditch to take shot with his second last bowl. I then drew shot with my last leaving Steve about half a metre to draw to stay alive but he fell centimetres short, resulting in my best win to that date. I was only 24 and could proudly add the Golden Nugget to my list of achievements.

I followed up by winning the Logan City Classic Pairs in October, so four major titles in one year made 1994 a year to remember.

8

Bowled Over

I met my wife Karen (surname Lewis back then) at the Playroom Nightclub in Tallebudgera in June 1990. I was 21 and she was 19.

It was a live band venue that I used to go to with my mates. I saw some great bands there including Crowded House, Noiseworks, Jimmy Barnes, Dragon, 1927 and INXS. The club had two levels, a big stage, a big dance floor, cheap drinks and crammed the patrons in, sometimes up to 3500 people. One night, I asked the manager for a job and he agreed to try me out as a 'glassie'. So I started working one or two nights a week and that grew to four to five nights a week. I was paid $10 an hour. I would start work at 8.30pm and sometimes finish as late (or early) as 5am, which allowed me to play tournaments and practise during the day, even though I was pretty tired.

The night I met Karen, Johnny Diesel (as he was then) was playing and while I was working I noticed her across the room having a night out with her girlfriends. The flower girl came around at about midnight and I asked her to take a yellow rose over to Karen.

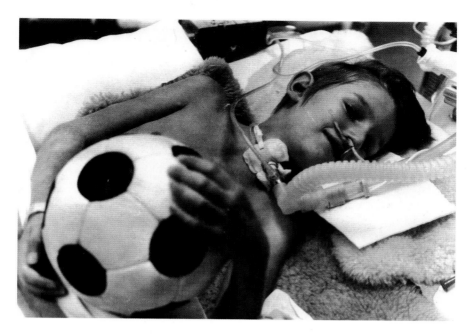

Intensive Care Unit, Royal Children's Hospital Brisbane, 1978.
Clutching the soccer ball I won in a Sunday Mail competition.

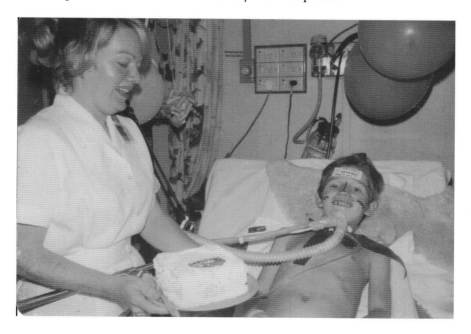

My 9th birthday in the Intensive Care Unit.
Unfortunately I couldn't eat the cake!

An outing in the park opposite the Royal Children's Hospital with Dad, my two sisters: Katrina (L) and Bronwyn and my favourite toy dog.

Slow road to recovery.
Learning to walk again by pushing a lawn-mower and wearing caliphers on my parent's farm.

On my bike...still wearing calliphers.

My first junior singles trophy; the School Boys Title, 1984 at Brunswick Heads Bowling Club.

Receiving the trophy for the Queensland State Junior Singles, Pine Rivers Bowling Club, 1986

The 'Teen' machine after winning the Gold Coast Winter Carnival fours competition at Tweed Heads Bowling Club, 1988. (L-R) Brett Walton, myself, Rob Parella, Darren Vardy.

In front of the main score board after defeating Rob Parella in the Master of Masters at Coolangatta Bowls Club, 1993.

With Trevor Morris, my skip when I debuted for a Queensland team in1989.

Receiving the trophy for the Gold Coast District Pairs Championship with Robbie Dobbins, 1992.

The Australian under 25 team that toured Hong Kong in1993.
(back row) Adam Jeffrey, Peter Harris, myself
(front row) Adam Gleeson, Steve Glasson.

The Queensland State Team in Tasmania, 1990.

Receiving my first major cheque as winner of the Golden Nugget at Tweed Heads Bowling Club, 1994.

The 1995 Queensland State Fours Champions and 1996 Australian Champions. (L-R) Steve Anderson, Steve Glasson, myself, Robbie Dobbins.

Our wedding day. We were married in the Burleigh Heads Catholic Church opposite the Burleigh Heads Bowls Club.

I then summoned up the courage to walk over and introduce myself and we hit it off straight away. When I told her I played bowls she was a bit shocked. She thought it was an oldies game but she adapted and was incredibly supportive in those early days when there was not a lot of money.

We got married on 19 November 1994 at Burleigh Heads Catholic Church, next to the Burleigh Heads Bowls Club. I went to the bowls club about an hour before the church for a couple of looseners — beers not bowls with my best man, Drew, and future brother-in-law, Chris.

We had about 100 people attend our wedding with quite a few bowlers, including Rob Parella, Bob Purcell and Robbie Dobbins. The only time I've been more nervous was the first time I played for Australia. It was a big commitment and I got even more twitchy when I saw Karen walk down the aisle. She looked incredible in her white wedding gown with its long train.

We had a bowls honeymoon. I had won the Queensland State Pairs and had to go to the Australian Pairs Championships in Queanbeyan, ACT. We went there for our honeymoon and then continued on to the Snowy Mountains. The bowls? We lost in section play. My mind was on other things. We hired a car as soon as we lost and we were out of there. We stayed at Lake Crackenback at the Novotel, with a balcony overlooking the water. I remember seeing the trout swimming around in the lake and then getting comfortable around the open fire at night.

We did it tough for the first few years, living in a granny flat at Karen's parents' place in Palm Beach. When I was away and

Karen was working we had built-in babysitters. Karen's parents, Mary and Ron, were excellent; they gave us the opportunity to get started. I'd put my tournament money in the bank and we saved money by not having to pay big rent. I think we only paid something like $50 a week, which allowed us to get a deposit and a home loan.

There was no money in the sport at the time. Even Australian team members only received $50 per day! I was still working at the Playroom. I was there for five years, working my way up from glassie to head glassie. We would have about 20 glassies on big nights and I organised the rosters and also did a bit of bar work. When the council refused to renew the lease, the Playroom closed down and the building was demolished for a park. It was sad to see it go as it was a big part of my early bowling career, my employment, my social life and where I met my wife. I have great memories of the place.

After the Playroom I did some part-time courier work before I started working as a gardener/greenkeeper at Tweed Heads Bowls Club. That's why I left Coolangatta. I worked 25 hours a week and they would roster me so I could play bowls. I could take time off to bowl and had a job when I wasn't bowling, so it was perfect.

The year I joined, Tweed Heads won the Division 1 pennant for the first time in 20 years. We had won three in a row at Coolangatta so that made it four in a row for me. I dragged some players there with me, including Andrew Waddell, who I won the state pairs with in 1994. He also came to Tweed Heads because of a job opportunity for his lawn-mowing business. John Whyper was the head greenkeeper then and still is. He was my boss and a member of the team that won the flag that year.

After about three years I left to go to South Tweed who had offered me a better position. At Tweed Heads I was only paid for the hours I worked whereas South Tweed Heads put me on a salary, which gave me a bit of security and allowed us to get a home loan. I had more work and it was more flexible. At Tweed Heads I could only work in the day but at South I could work nights as well in the club and was guaranteed 35 hours a week.

Throughout all of this, Karen had been fantastic. I can hardly find the words to describe how amazing she has been … 'unbelievable' and 'outstanding' would be a couple. I've spent a lot of time away, and she has allowed me to share my commitment to her, the woman I love, with my commitment to bowls, the game I love, and she wanted me to be the best I could be.

9

Singled Out for Debut

In February 1995, Robbie Dobbins rang me late in the afternoon and said, 'We need you to get here and play.'

I was blown away. Robbie was the Australian coach and the team was playing a Test series against New Zealand. It was unbelievable and I was stoked at the time. It was a huge honour to be asked to play.

I wasn't originally in the team but on the second day's play in wet conditions, Aussie skip Steve Anderson played a drive and tore his groin muscle. He couldn't go on so Robbie Dobbins asked if I could make the two-and-a-half-hour drive to replace him for the next day's play. There was no time for any players from interstate to make the trip. I had just been selected in the greater Australian squad of 20 players at the time, so the call-up was a surprise. To get a chance due to injury doesn't happen often in bowls, and I was pretty excited about getting the opportunity.

I drove up alone in my Datsun Sunny, which was probably the furthest I'd ever driven at that stage, arriving at about 8.30pm. I went straight to bed when I got there but I don't think

I slept too well.

I went to Noosa Bowls Club early the next morning and had a roll-up before a team meeting. There was a lot of 'Welcome to the team,' 'Thanks for filling in,' 'It's great to have you,' and 'Now let's go out and win!' I came into the second of the three test series as lead. My teammates were Dave Stockholm, Cameron Curtis, Rex Johnson, Geoff Sutcliffe and of course Steve Anderson. The morning matches in the second test were triples and pairs. I played triples with Dave Stockholm and Rex Johnson. The nerves kicked in just like with my Queensland debut but I had played a lot of competitive bowls by then so I settled down really well after a couple of ends. We won both the triples and pairs. In the afternoon I played fours, again in the lead. It was a rainy afternoon and I felt more relaxed as having got through the first game with a win was a confidence booster. Apparently I played really well, although I can't remember a lot. Robbie Dobbins said it was an outstanding effort, filling in at the last minute. The team had been practising for days, but I managed to play well without the benefit of the practice sessions. Most importantly, we won the series 2–1.

I've played in the national sides championships 18 times now, but I will never forget the exhilaration of being picked to play for Australia that first time. What made it all the better was that it was just like getting a call from a mate.

One of the greatest honours of my career, and certainly the greatest at that point in time, was to be selected over Rob Parella to play singles for Australia at the Pacific Championships in Dunedin, New Zealand, in November 1995.

I was thrilled to pieces when I was selected and all I could think for the next couple of months was, *Geez, I just wanna do well*. I was really keen to continue playing singles for Australia after New Zealand. It was to be a whole new ball game, playing against players that I'd never played before and also playing on grass that I'd never played on before. The grass was soft and green and I therefore expected it to run really slowly, but it was deceptively fast. On the Gold Coast, when the greens are hard and brown they run fast, and when they're green they're slow. But in Dunedin the greens were green and yet they ran fast. It was a case of telling my brain not to believe what it saw. Fortunately we had six days of preparation before the tournament, which gave me a chance to get my head around the new surface and get into a groove.

I was keen to justify the selectors' faith in me and progressed confidently through the early rounds, beating the Canadian, David Duncalf, 25–13 and the American, Pat Fagan, 25–2. I then had a lapse in the third round, losing to the Western Samoan bowler Fa'manu Tausisi Amituona'i, but regained composure to convincingly defeat Makoto Yamada from Japan 25–3 in a morning game, and in the afternoon had another result against Norfolk Island's Dan Yager 25–5. In my final round I beat the Papua New Guinean representative 25–10 to book a place in the final the next day against the formidable unbeaten home-town favourite from New Zealand, Rowan Brassey.

I knew I had to fly the flag for Australia as I was the last hope of the men's team, winning a gold medal at the Games after the men's fours fell in an upset to Fiji.

In the early ends Brassey outplayed me and was drawing red-hot to go to an 8–2 lead. Robbie Dobbins then approached me on the bank and suggested I change my tactics. What he wanted me to do was to drive at Brassey's first bowl if he was close to the jack rather than try to outdraw him. My aggression payed off and threw Brassey off his rhythm. During the match I killed four ends and hit 13 of my 16 drives. I literally drove him off the green, and if not for my driving he would have walked right over me. The game went down to the wire with scores tied at 23–23 before the 27th and final end. On the last end, I started with a close bowl but Brassey drew inside me for a resting toucher and then added another shot. I had no option but to drive, and sent jack and my toucher into the ditch, leaving Brassy a couple of metres to draw, but he had a concentration lapse and fell short. I then had one bowl to draw a gold medal. The bowl was smooth out of the hand with a touch of weight. It turned out to be just the right touch as it pulled up centimetres short of the ditch to give me two shots and the match 25–23. You beauty! I threw my cap into the air as I celebrated winning my first singles international gold medal.

I attribute a large part of my success in New Zealand to Robbie Dobbins, who was still the Australian coach and a great mentor and friend. He was like a footy coach, inspiring confidence in his players, encouraging us to play as a team and back one another up. The positive team attitude he instilled in me added a lot to my game. Robbie also had the knack of making us all feel relaxed even though we were playing for Australia. He also encouraged us to respect the opposition and sit down and have a couple of beers and a chat after a game.

Indoors in the UK

In January 1996 I departed for my first trip to the UK for the World Indoor Championships. January is the middle of winter in the UK and I'd never been to a place that cold. Coming straight from the Gold Coast, it was a real shock.

On the trip, I was sharing a room with Ian Schuback in a hotel about 400 metres from the venue, the Preston Guild Hall. It was on the fringe of the town centre and to get to the venue we had to walk through the bus terminal and then across a big open park, and I'd be freezing because it was about four or five degrees. One night there was very heavy snowfall, about a foot and a half of snow overnight, which was pretty much unheard of as they hadn't had snow like that for years. When I went outside, I couldn't believe it. It was the first time I'd seen snow. I thought, 'How good's this stuff?' It was really cold but pretty to see. I was in the car park outside the hotel entrance, and it was all snow — snow halfway up the car wheels, so nothing was moving. The place was at a standstill.

Then Mark McMahon, who was playing for Hong Kong at that time, and a couple of other players staying in the hotel did the only thing to do in the circumstances — have a snow fight! We were pegging snowballs at each other for about half an hour. I didn't realise that my fingers were wet, turning purple and shrinking from the cold. When I went back inside and rubbed my hands together to warm up, I realised that my wedding ring was not on my finger where it should be. Finding the ring would be like trying to find a needle in a haystack; with the snow outside there was no chance. When the snow melted a few days later, I searched the place for a few hours, but there was no sign of the ring.

I had to face the fact that I had managed to lose my wedding ring, but what was really worrying me was *How do I tell my wife I've lost my wedding ring?* I sweated for 24 hours before I told her. I ended up going to the same jewellery shop where we bought our rings and got them to make an exact replica.

I could not have wished for a better partner in the pairs than Ian Schuback. 'Shooey' had won this event eight years prior in 1988 with Jim Yates from Victoria and then repeated the feat two years later with Cameron Curtis.

I suddenly found myself mixing with some of the best players in the world, including Tony Allcock, Richard Corsie, Andy Thomson, David Gourlay and David Bryant. As the new kid on the block, I was obviously a bit nervous. I got better as each game went on, but Shooey was at the top of his game and helped me through the tournament.

At first the media in the UK was intrigued by my three-quarter-length stick and questioned if it gave me an unfair advantage on the green. The truth is that it does give me some assistance, otherwise I wouldn't use it, but I would dearly love to be rid of it. I often practice without it, but after about a dozen ends my right leg starts to get a bit sore and my balance gets worse. It puts that much added pressure on my good leg that I couldn't get through a match without it. But the stick is also a hindrance as it can get in the way when I drive. I have a tendency to swing across my body in the driving action because I am leaning on the stick.

Our first match on the portable rink in Preston Guild Hall was a hard-fought four-set victory over the Welsh pair, Garfield Phillips and Cliff Williams, and we backed that up with another tough four-set win over Mark McMahon and Ian Taylor. Those two matches gave us a chance to bowl ourselves into form on the carpet and gave us confidence for our semi-final showdown against the reigning pairs champions, Richard Corsie and Alex Marshall. It was another tight match, but we claimed a last bowl victory against the Scots to secure a finals berth.

In the final we were up against former Indoor champions Andy Thomson and Gary Smith of England. We got off to a shaky start in the first set and were trailing 5–3 until we won two shots in succession to take the set. England bounced back to take the second set and we knew we were in for a good old Australia versus England battle, which seems to happen no matter what the sport when our two countries meet. The third set was a real cliff-hanger. We were tied at 6–6 and two shots down with two back bowls when Shooey played an up-shot with his last, picking up the kitty and the shot after a measure. In the final set at 5–4 up, Shooey again pulled out a corker, turning out Thomson's bowl for three shots and the title, 7–5, 2–7, 7–6, 4–7, 7–4. It was Shooey's third World Indoor Championship and he told the media that he wanted to win it for 'Spike' (that's me), so that I would know what it is like to win a world title. Thanks, mate! It was definitely the biggest win of my career to that date. I was really thankful to Ian for inviting me to play the World Indoors with him as it was a stepping-stone for me to playing bowls in the UK. I gained recognition as the new Aussie guy to take the English bowls scene by storm. My reputation in the UK was enhanced by winning the Welsh Masters Singles one year after the World Indoor Pairs victory.

When I played the Welsh Masters it was my first time in Wales, and I was a little bit overawed. Again, I found myself in the company of the world's best, but I didn't let the situation get the better of me.

From the first match I played I got into the groove and I don't think people could believe how well I was playing. Even I couldn't believe how well I was bowling! When I started knocking them off one by one, I began to realise that I was in red-hot form and could beat anyone. To this day, it's one of the best tournaments I have ever competed in. I played consistently well every game and I am forever grateful to the locals who started to get behind me even though they didn't know too much about me. I'd won the Indoor pairs with Ian Schuback the year before, so people had heard of me, but to come out and win the Welsh Masters started a love affair with the event and the crowd.

It was my first major singles win in the UK and what was most gratifying was to gain the respect of my peers, who all graciously acknowledged that I had been the best player at the tournament.

The March issue of Bowls International magazine had an article by David Rhys Jones with the headline: 'Aussie Ace Spikes UK's Big Guns'. The article went on to say, 'Kelvin "Spike" Kerkow, the 27-year-old Australian who carries a walking stick onto the rink, turned on the style to win the CIS Insurance-sponsored Welsh Masters in Llanelli. No less an authority than David Bryant described Kerkow's performance as "the best exhibition of singles play I've ever seen", while Welsh stalwart Jim Morgan, who won a gold medal at the 1986 Commonwealth Games, agreed: "He was awesome – I've never seen a better game of singles than the final between Kelvin and John Price." Kerkow swept aside new Welsh champion Robert Weale, twice world indoor champion Andy Thomson and Commonwealth champion Richard Corsie on his way to the final, where he found the holder, Wales' John Price, in good form on his favourite rink. But it was the Aussie, drawing, trailing and firing with equal skill, who mopped up 7–4, 7–4, 7–5, the only question being how on earth did Price manage to score 13 shots against a man in such inspired form. The world-class 12-man field included seven world indoor champions … but there was no doubt that Kerkow was the star of the show.'

RESULTS

First round:

Ian Schuback (Australia) bt Gareth Williams (Wales) 7–6, 7–3;

Tony Allcock (England) bt Jeremy Henry (Ireland) 3–7, 7–6, 7–4;

Steve Rees (Wales) bt Hugh Duff (Scotland) 7–1, 7–3;

Kelvin Kerkow (Australia) bt Robert Weale (Wales) 7–0, 5–7, 7–0.

Quarter finals:

John Price (Wales) bt Schuback 7–4, 1–7, 7–6;

David Gourlay (Scotland) bt Allcock 7–0, 7–3;

Richard Corsie (Scotland) bt Rees 7–2, 7–3;

Kerkow bt Andy Thomson (England) 7–1, 2–7, 7–6.

Semi-finals:

Price bt Gourlay 7–6, 4–7, 7–2;

Kerkow bt Corsie 7–2, 5–7, 7–0.

Final:

Kerkow bt Price 7–4, 7–4, 7–5.

I love playing in the UK and I really enjoy playing on the carpet. It's a very true surface and you don't have to worry about the wind or other outside conditions. It's a pure contest of skill where one player is matched against the other in identical conditions. It tends to result in tight games that suit TV; a lot of events in the UK are televised on BBC2 with a viewing audience of up to 10 million people for a major final. I have never got over the sensation of playing in a televised match and then going down to the local pub where people would come up to me while I'm having a beer and say things like, 'Well played, I saw you on TV,' or 'Fantastic to see you giving our English bowlers a run for their money.' It's a great way to meet the locals without having the pressure of being in the Australian team and having specific curfews and training times. I'm running on my own steam, so I can prepare how I want to prepare without being given a strict schedule. But, don't worry, I still put in the hard yards and in the UK I'd often practice from midnight for a couple of hours or get up and practise from 4am to 7am. The reason I would keep these odd practice hours is that there's a lot of scheduled matches in the World Championships over three weeks, but there's only one portable rink and there can obviously only be one match at a time, with each match lasting about two hours. So, with a field of 48 for the men's singles, there are 24 matches in the first round and probably only four matches a day. As a result, there may be three or four days in the tournament when I am not playing. This has been one of my downfalls in the men's singles, because I like to get into the rhythm of a tournament: play, win, and continue playing the next day. One of the reasons for my success in the World Indoor pairs is that the games were played over four consecutive days.

Because of the games being played during the day, the only time to practise is after 9.30 at night until 9.30 in the morning. Generally, if you get up at 7am or 8am, you have to share the rink with two or three other guys, whereas if you go at 1am or 4am, everyone's in bed so you've got the rink all to yourself. That's been a bit of a trade secret of mine.

The UK has become a home away from home for me. I'm sponsored by Taylors, and the Taylors factory is in Glasgow, Scotland. They store all my bowls for me, probably about five sets of bowls that I regularly use — they're all Taylor Ace or Taylor Vector bowls. They probably turn a bit wider than the bowls we use in Queensland; however, they can be effective on the slower greens in the southern states. They're definitely nice to use on an indoor carpet synthetic.

One of the quirky things about the World Bowls Tour is that the portable rink is a blue carpet, and you've got to use green or red bowls. We have been told not to use any other colour bowls as the green and red show up best against the blue on television. If you're at the top of the draw you use red bowls and green if you are in the bottom half. My red and green sets are exactly the same and it doesn't normally worry me to change, but psychologically I prefer the red. If I'm the defending champion, it means I have the number one spot at the top of the draw and so I use red bowls; therefore, reds are associated with being the bowls of the 'top dog'.

The only real superstition I have when playing bowls is that I like to wear the same socks if I'm winning, especially in indoor tournaments. I don't know why — it just feels nice, just a bit of a lucky charm, and I don't wash them, either!

11

Triumphs and Disappointments

While I had adapted well to the UK and playing indoors, there was nothing really to compare to playing on one of the best outdoor greens in the world at Tweed Heads in Australia's greatest singles event, The Golden Nugget. In the 1997 event I managed to make it through to the final despite going down to Mark Jacobsen in the final round of sectional play, 25–22. Mark and I finished on equal tournament points, but fortunately for me I was 9 shots up overall and went into the final against Andrew Waddell.

It was a really tight match played in front of a capacity crowd of 3000 people. After 10 ends we were tied at 9–9, but Andrew jumped away to lead 20–11 by the 17th end. I pegged him back, winning single shots on 5 of the next 6 ends and then continued to apply the pressure going to a 24-21 lead. On the second last end, Andrew picked up 3 to tie and on the last end he was forced to drive to take out my shot bowl, but missed and I had my second Golden Nugget!

I was as proud as punch to be one of only three players to have won the Nugget twice, joining the late Ken Williams

(1986, 1990) and Ian Schuback (1987, 1992).

While I seemed to be having a charmed career, things did not always go my way. I had my heart set on playing for my country in the 1998 Commonwealth Games in Malaysia, and missing out on selection was one of my greatest disappointments.

We travelled to Malaysia for the trials, which were held in really humid conditions on new greens that were running ridiculously slow at nine or ten seconds. This was quite a shock after playing on the fast greens of the Gold Coast. But then, that's exactly why we trialled in Malaysia, as these were the conditions the team would be confronted with in the Games.

I simply didn't adapt to the heavy greens. I was the Australian number one at that time but I played the worst out of everyone at those trials and I only have myself to blame. Unfortunately I had the wrong bowls — I needed old bowls with a lot of bias, but I brought the bowls I had been using in Queensland. What a mistake that turned out to be, but I guess I have to put it down to inexperience. I was probably playing better than anyone else in Australia in the six months leading up to the four-day trials, so it was a bit of a shock when I was told I had missed out. The Commonwealth Games were still three months down the track and I thought that would have given me enough time to prepare.

Some time later, the chairman of selectors, Charlie Frost, told me it was one of the hardest decisions he ever had to make: 'You were the first pick before we took off to go there,' he told me.

The other guys trialled well, and Brett Duprez was selected

instead of me. He did really well, winning the gold medal in the men's pairs with Mark Jacobsen. However, Steve Glasson was unlucky to just miss out on a medal in the singles and the triples also failed to medal.

The disappointment of missing out on the Games in Malaysia was forgotten when I was selected for the pairs in the 2002 Commonwealth Games in Manchester, England. The trials were played in the UK on slow greens, but I had learnt my lesson and trialled well. However, the weather rained on our parade. None of us were prepared for the continuous rain and saturated greens we had to contend with.

The Manchester greens were purpose-built for the games and had been laid only twelve months prior so the grass had not taken strong root. When I played against South Africa in the quarter finals of the pairs with Andrew Smith from South Australia, the greens were so heavy that my drive did not reach the ditch! There was a sheet of water covering the rink and it was like playing on a muddy, wet field. The next day the rink was ruled unplayable and closed. A day too late by my reckoning!

Of course we were disappointed at being beaten by South Africa and missing out on a medal; however, neither Andrew nor I had ever experienced such appalling conditions.

The bowls team at those games was the worst performed of any Australian Commonwealth Games bowls side before or since. The story for me at the Games went from bad to worse.

I was rooming in the athletes' village with Gary Willis who played in the fours. The rule was that all rubbish had to be removed from the room on departure and whilst we tidied up our room, we placed the 20 or so sports drinks bottles on the windowsill and had a small pile of magazines and newspapers neatly stacked in a corner of the room. We didn't think it was going to be a problem; however, when Geoff Oakley, the team manager came into the room for an inspection he wasn't impressed and he submitted an official report to Bowls Australia saying that we had broken the rules. Somehow, the media got hold of the story and all of a sudden we were hearing reports that we had trashed the room, ripped wallpaper off the walls (when there wasn't any) and ripped up the carpet (when there were only floorboards).

When I returned home to the Gold Coast I was confronted by news reporters wanting to know more about this supposed 'room trashing'. I couldn't believe how exaggerated the story had become. Bowls Australia didn't take too kindly to the report, and fair enough, we had broken the rule by leaving drink bottles and reading material in the room and I was happy to plead guilty to that. I had to front a committee set up by Bowls Australia, and Gary and I were given a 12-month suspended good behaviour sentence. Gary actually got into more trouble than me as he was also cited for drinking into the wee hours after the fours team lost their quarter final to Wales, including dropping an eight on one end. Apparently he and Adam Jeffrey polished off a few bottles of red wine with accompanying laughter and loud conversation, and as our floor was directly above the boxing team a report was submitted that the Bowls team was disruptive to the Boxing team. And to top it off, the Hockey Team complained that we were a bunch of drunks.

Let's just say it was a disappointing Commonwealth Games!

Another disappointment in my career was that, as the reigning Welsh Masters Single champion of 1997, I would have liked to defend my title the following year. However, as the tournament was not then part of the World Bowls Tour, I would have had to pay my way over and that just wasn't a possibility at the time. When the tournament achieved World Tour status I was not ranked in the world Top 16 and therefore did not receive an invitation. Nevertheless, I was naturally keen to play so I entered the qualifying rounds in Australia. The Welsh International Open takes one qualifier from Australia, so I paid my £100 entry fee along with 31 other hopefuls in September 2003 and won my way through the knockout competition undefeated to secure my berth in the Welsh Masters for February 2004.

The day I walked back into the bowls centre in Llanelli after not being there for seven years, it was déjà vu; the same smiling faces that were there when I won the previous time were welcoming me and wishing me the best for the tournament. My first game was even on the same end rink where I won in 1997.

In the fist round of the 2004 Welsh Masters I knocked out Alex Marshall, which was a good scalp as Alex had only three weeks before won the world singles title for a record-equalling third time. I was back in my 1997 groove, and thought to myself, 'Hey, I've just beaten the world champion … I can do this again!' The crowd got right behind me and it was just like playing at home. The Welsh people opened their hearts to me, maybe because I'd won there before and had to fight my way back to play there again. Crowd support has always made me feel more relaxed and helps me in my self-belief. When I'm on a roll and the crowd's cheering me on and I'm playing well, things just seem to go my way.

I continued in winning form against Mark Royal in the second round, Stuart Airey in the quarter final, and Neil Furman in the semi-final to book a berth in the final against England's Andy Thomson. I took great delight in winning the final in a tiebreak 10–7, 6–11, 2–1 to win my second Welsh Masters Singles title seven years after winning it for the first time. I had to win nine consecutive games, including qualifiers in Australia, and then beat the best in the world to do so. Naturally, this win gave me a great deal of satisfaction.

Twelve Beers by 12 O'Clock

In 2000 the Australian Bowls squad travelled to Johannesburg to trial for the World Bowls championship. After the experience of the slow greens at the Malaysian Commonwealth Games it was decided to trial on the greens in South Africa. We had three-day trials at a couple of clubs in Johannesburg, where the greens were a bit rough and quite slow, running at about eleven seconds. The eight-man squad was to be trimmed to a five-man team (the World Bowls is always a five-man team) but it wasn't to be announced until we returned to Australia.

Before the trials, most of the guys had decided that the trip to South Africa was a perfect opportunity to visit the Kruger National Park. So we arranged a five-day tour starting the day after the trials. Our one rule for the trip was that there would be no discussions whatsoever in relation to bowls. We wouldn't be talking about the previous days' trials, no talk about the team — it was just going be a genuine five-day camp and a good time, sitting back and relaxing, taking in the wildlife and all that sort of jazz.

We all piled into a mini-bus with a trailer at the back and

our own driver. On the safari was Steve Glasson, Chris Young, Adam Jeffrey, Rex Johnson, Brett Duprez and myself. Kevin Walsh and Marc Jacobsen had decided to fly straight home after the trial, so it was just the six of us. We left at about 10 o'clock the morning after the last trial, and we headed straight to the nearest liquor shop to load up. We bought about twelve cartons of Castle Lager and half a dozen bottles of spirits. I also bought four bottles of what they call 'Cane and Coke' because it was cheap (about $8 a bottle). It's a clear spirit that looks like Bacardi and is actually made from sugar cane. When you mix it with Coke it tastes like you're just drinking Coke but it gets you pissed!

Once fully stocked we headed for the Kruger National Park. We drove about five or six hours the first day and stayed overnight in a motel where we enjoyed a few drinks, and the next day set off again with about a three-hour drive still ahead of us. That morning we decided that our aim was to each have twelve beers by 12 o'clock. Every 40 miles or so we'd pull up to visit a small roadside market where the locals were selling elephant and giraffe carvings and other souvenirs. The revelation for us was Chris Young, a quiet guy from country Victoria who just played his bowls and kept to himself on the trip who really came out of his shell. He completed his twelve beers and at the next roadside stop there happened to be a line of ten dancing girls and a group of percussionists on bongos and other instruments belting out tribal rhythms as part of the attraction. We were treated to the Chris Young show as he proceeded to dance up a storm with the scantily clad dancers. We couldn't believe our eyes. He was so smashed and having such a great time that we eventually had to drag him back to the bus…and it had only just turned 12 o'clock!

We finally arrived at the campsite in the middle of the Kruger National Park surrounded by steel fencing with large four-person thatched huts in the middle. Each night we had a barbecue within the confines of the fence to the sounds of all sorts of wild animals including hyenas, lions and elephants to name just a few that lurked in the darkness.

We had about twelve cartons of Castle and on the first night in camp we really hit it hard. Chris Young showed us how to drink a can of beer in five seconds by punching a hole in the bottom of the can and lifting the lid, which snaps the top of the can causing the beer to run straight down his throat. So we all gave it a try but I think the fastest we could manage was eleven or twelve seconds a can. But Chris was unreal, and because he was showing us he knocked them down one after another — he was a real party animal. The hyenas were howling and growling just outside the fence. The smell of the barbecue was driving them crazy and they were chomping to get at us. But as the night went on, our howling was just as loud as theirs and it was becoming difficult to tell which were the wildest animals.

Somehow the night ended in a shaving cream fight and you wouldn't believe it, but I actually lost my wedding ring — again — in a grassy area in the compound. We were play-fighting and the ring came off, but I didn't realise until the next morning when we were having breakfast. We all went outside and got on our hands and knees looking for my wedding ring, but unlike in the snow in England, after about half an hour we found it.

That next morning were all a bit worse for wear, but on the

second day we left at 5am to give ourselves the best chance of seeing animals in the wild. From the safety of the minibus we saw lions lying just meters away, as well as crocodiles, buffaloes, zebras and thousands of springboks. It was truly an amazing experience and to get away from bowls for a few days and go to the Kruger National Park is one of the best things I've ever done.

After reading about our South African safari, I don't want you to think that the guys on that trip are a bunch of 'pisspots'. While I like a drink when celebrating or having a trip with the boys, I personally don't drink before any competition that I play in. Even if it's just a club pennant game, I normally just have a Coke before I play, and I'll have a few beers after the game. But I never drink while I play. The only exception is if it's a social 'barefoot' bowls day. I think alcohol will certainly affect your game, because it is a touch game, a game of rhythm and technique. With alcohol in your system your game is going to suffer. One or two beers might make you feel a little bit more relaxed, and you see a lot of reasonably competitive pennant players in division 1 or 2 that will have a couple of beers before a game, but if you're having four or five before you start, there's no doubt that it's going to adversely affect your game.

From the Kruger National Park we headed straight back to Johannesburg Airport and flew home, and when the team was announced I learnt that I wasn't selected. I think I trialled quite well and was probably the sixth man. The team selected was similar to the team selected for the 1998 Commonwealth Games, because the greens in South Africa were as slow as those in Malaysia, and at that time, playing on slow greens was not my strong suit. I made sure that I improved on that area of my game to make sure I was selected for the 2004 World Championships on the slow greens in Scotland.

The team of Brett Duprez, Rex Johnson, Adam Jeffrey, Steve Glasson and Mark Jacobsen performed very well, winning the 2000 championships and proving they were definitely the best bowlers for the conditions.

13

Slow Going in Scotland

I've always played indoor tournaments in the UK, except for 2004 when I played for Australia in the World Bowls championships, the 'Olympics of Lawn Bowls', in Scotland. The Australian Men's team, who had recently been named the 'Jackaroos', were defending the WM Leonard Trophy they won for the first time in 2000 in South Africa. Teams from 24 countries competed in all four disciplines: pairs and triples in the first week and singles and fours in the second week.

Our team, comprising Steve Glasson, Kevin Walsh, Brett Duprez, Michael Wilks and myself, arrived a week early to make sure we got plenty of practice on slow greens. We had high expectations of retaining the team trophy and winning gold in at least one or two disciplines.

Although we did get a lot of practice in the lead-up and were made to feel at home at the clubs who hosted us, we were not fully prepared for how slow the greens were to play at the Northfiled Bowls Complex in Ayr.

We made a horror start, losing three of our four matches on the opening day. We lost both pairs games and one of our triples in atrocious conditions. There was a howling wind and rain lashed down on us. In the pairs, Duprez and Walsh suffered a surprise 17–13 loss to Namibia in the first round and then a crushing 16-shot defeat to the English pair. They were then knocked out of contention after losing to Ireland the following day. Our only win came in the opening round of the triples in which Glasson, myself and Wilks beat Samoa 20–11, but we then had a four-shot shock defeat against Brazil. Neither our form nor the conditions improved much the following day when we were beaten by the United States 14–15, before prevailing over Swaziland 16–11. We needed to beat South Africa to qualify for the medal rounds.

We managed to get our act together against South Africa after being 6–0 down after two ends. What really saved our bacon was a huge seven count on the 15th end to help secure a 17–15 win. This advanced Australia into the medal rounds, involving two sections of six, from which the two winners play off for the gold medal.

We made a confidence-boosting start in medal rounds with a convincing 17–10 win over Hong Kong. Just when we thought we were back on track, we were given a bowling lesson on slow greens by Scotland, who belted us 27–6. Coach Robbie Dobbins said at the time: 'Scotland played the conditions perfectly. They beat us man for man right down the line. We just couldn't score and really had no answers.'

With our confidence in tatters, we then went down to Zimbabwe by seven shots and we ended up finishing a lowly fourth in our section.

We headed into the second week looking to salvage some

pride, with Steve Glasson playing in the singles and Brett Duprez, Kevin Walsh, Michael Wilks and myself contesting the fours. Both Steve and the fours got off to a flying start, proceeding through to the medal rounds undefeated. Steve then showed his true fighting spirit by clawing his way back from 14–20 down against Welshman Jason Greenslade to win 21–20, but suffered a setback when Fiji's Caucau Turagabeci came from 20–9 down to win 21–20. However, this setback did not stop Steve proceeding to the final along with the fours, who entered the gold medal match without a loss.

After Ireland took an early lead in the fours final, we made a late charge, picking up four shots on the final end, but went down by one shot, 19–18. After a disastrous first week for the pairs and triples, the fours only lost one match, and that was by one shot, to take the silver medal.

The highlight of the World Bowls Championships was definitely Steve Glasson being crowned world singles champion after defeating the reigning world number one, Scotland's Alex Marshall, by six shots. Scores were tied on four occasions during the match and after 17 ends the players were still tied at 15–15 before Steve made his match-winning move from the 18th end, collecting six shots over four ends for a 21–15 result. It was Steve's first gold medal at a major international event as a singles representative, and it was a sweet victory, erasing the memory of his loss at the Johannesburg World Championships four years earlier.

On completion of the tournament, Australian coach Robbie Dobbins assessed the team performance and also had some interesting things to say about why we didn't perform up to expectations in the first week in Scotland. I pretty much agree with his analysis and it provides food for thought for future Australian teams playing in the northern hemisphere.

Basically, Robbie concluded that we experienced the same difficulties that Australian teams have always had whenever competing at elite outdoor bowls competitions in the northern hemisphere. The first difficulty is in players not being able to play consistent lines. Most elite Australian players use an imaginary line for grass. This is fine on Australian greens, which are firm and level to the degree of millimetres, and a difference of one inch in grass line will not appreciably affect the finishing position of the bowl. However, in the northern hemisphere, the greens are not normally as well-prepared as those in Australia and are often soft, unlevelled, and every rink is entirely different, with changes in the degree of tracking at different lengths of the rink. On these greens, an inch of difference in grass line can alter the finishing position of a bowl by a metre or more.

The second difficulty is that the Australian player is taught from when they first begin to play bowls not to cross the centre line of the jack. We are conditioned to drawing to the jack, as our greens are receptive to being able to play the perfect bowl and we develop the skills to play this type of game.

In the northern hemisphere, however, the greens will not allow this perfection; the good players in these countries are conditioned to drawing through the jack and they are very seldom wide. We usually try to draw the perfect shot with the result of finishing far too often short of the head. The main advantage of the northern hemisphere-type game is that playing to cross over the line and slightly through the head increases the chance of getting lucky and decreases the amount of short and ineffective bowls.

The third and biggest difficulty we face in the northern hemisphere is when playing four-by-four pairs and three-bowl triples. Both of these disciplines are rarely played by our elite players in Australia, and in Robbie's opinion should never be played at the international level. These disciplines involve players having multiple bowls in succession, and when you combine this with the difficult tracking green conditions, it allows people who attack the head (no matter what the consequences) to be favoured with huge amounts of luck. The tactics needed in these types of games is entirely different from those normally used by our elite players; therefore, the skipper needs to be more of a tactical thinker than a good technical player.

Back on the Tour

I was fortunate enough to have a good year in 2004 on the World Bowls Tour and I was granted the very last invite to the World Indoor Pairs in the 2005 championships. I had the choice to pick anyone in the top 24 in the world who wasn't already paired up. Merv King was a current English international player and ranked 23, but none of the other UK players in the competition — including Alex Marshall, Paul Foster, Andy Thomson, Richard Corsie and David Gourlay — had asked him to play with them. I had met Merv before in an Australia-versus-England international test series in Australia and I had also met his fellow countryman, Billy Jackson, whom I had also played in an England International. The reason I finally asked Merv was that he was from the Norfolk county where the World Championships are held every year. Their home is at Potter's Leisure Resort in the small town of Hopton-on-Sea in Norfolk. Merv King lives about an hour away in Fakenham and he's the best bowler in the area. So when he played, whether singles or pairs, he would bring along a busload of supporters. And because I was his partner, they also supported me, whether

I was playing in the pairs or singles. I got to know a lot of his mates in his club, and I started to feel a bit like a local boy.

In the 2005 final we came up against the formidable pair of Greg Harlow from Cambridgeshire, England, and Jonathan Ross from Belfast, Ireland. Greg is one of the best indoor players going around in the UK and is an 'indoor specialist'. It was an exceptionally tight final, and we were absolutely thrilled to win both sets by two shots

Merv loves his red wine, especially Aussie reds, and I'm always taking him a couple of bottles when I travel to the UK. Merv also likes to celebrate a win. Unfortunately, when we won the World Indoors in 2005, I couldn't stay around to celebrate with him, because if I hadn't caught the flight that night I would have been stranded in England for another week, and I'd already been there three. Many flights over the previous week had been cancelled due to bad weather so there was a backlog of flights. The match finished at 5pm, Merv and I had a brief media session, and I gathered my bags from the locker-room knowing that, win or lose, I had to go straight to the airport. So I walked off the green after I'd won the title and left the venue within 20 minutes. I was in a car, dropped off at Heathrow and, being a gold class frequent flyer, waltzed straight through business check-in carrying my big championship glass-cup onto the plane. I had a few quiet wines on the plane to toast our victory, knowing that my pairs partner would be absolutely sloshed that night!

This win had a special significance for Merv. In the dressing room the morning before our first round match, he said to me, 'I've had a little bet with my wife, Suzanne, in regard to this tournament.' I said, 'What would that be?' He told me that he has three kids from his first relationship and that his wife, also has two, so they weren't planning to have any more. 'Mate,' he said, 'if I don't win this event, I've got to go and get the old cord chained up so we can't have any more kids. That's if I lose. But if I win, she's got to get it done!' So I guess Merv had two reasons to celebrate!

I only had a break of two weeks at home before I had to return to the UK to defend my Welsh International Singles title. There was no way I was going to have to play the qualifiers for the 2005 event!

Within days of arriving back in Australia, carrying my trophy, I was on a plane to Melbourne to help the Australian side win the Trans-Tasman series against New Zealand in freezing and wet conditions.

Then it was back to the airport for the long haul to the UK. Jamie Hill, who was also playing in the Trans-Tasman, was the New Zealand representative for the Welsh Masters; however, he had booked his flight to England via New Zealand and America. We were rooming together in Wales and while we left Melbourne at the same time, I arrived three hours before him. As soon as the Trans-Tasman finished, I rang Karen and said, 'Darl, you're gonna have to meet me in Brisbane because I'm flying back to England and this is the only way we can see each other.' I arrived in Brisbane at 10am, then flew out to England at 1pm — just long enough to have lunch with Karen in the airport.

I arrived at the venue in Wales at about 1pm and Jamie showed up at about 4pm. While I was playing my match the next day, Jamie had to play Les Gillett, a classy England International player, at 7.30 that evening. The players and officials at the event were shaking their heads in disbelief that we had travelled so far and gave ourselves so little time to recover. And they were right: it is tough to fly from one side of the world to the other and be relaxed enough to play good bowls. It normally takes me two or three days before my hands stop trembling and my eyes stop burning,

Jamie had quite a few pints of beer before his game and when it started he was shaking, his ankles were swollen from the long flight and his eyes were bloodshot. No one gave him a chance in hell — but he played unreal and won!

The next day I was still jet-lagged and didn't feel my best, but, inspired by Jamie, I also won. I made it through to the semi-final where I fought back from a set down to overcome Scotland's world champion Paul Foster 6–8, 6–5, 2–0 and I was through to the final against Welshman Robert Weale.

The crowd was understandably a little more subdued in their support for me, as Robert is the local hero and obviously one of the best players in Wales. Despite the home support for him, I still had enough support to help me cruise through the first set of the final and then survive a nail-biting second to become the first player to win the Welsh Masters Singles title for the third time.

I've given some thought to why I've been so successful in the Welsh Masters and other World Bowls Tour events. As well as having crowd support and being able to get in the groove and draw confidently on the carpet, I put it down to being an attacking player. I believe I've had one of the best drives in the game over the last six or seven years, and I've used it tactically in the big singles games that I've played. I've driven to destroy the head or take out a shot bowl and I don't think that English players are used to that. In the UK they play 'swingers' or weighted shots, whereas when I went over there I just went full blast, straight down the middle and I don't think they were used to that. So it made them play their game a bit differently from what they were used to. Perhaps they started to play a bit more defensively against me, putting a bowl around the back and not building up too big a target around the kitty.

When a batsman scores a century whenever he plays on a certain ground, he usually says he wishes he could take that wicket with him wherever he plays. Well, that is what happens when I play the indoor circuit in the UK. It's the same piece of carpet that we play on in each venue — they just pack it up and put it in a truck and install it at the next venue. It can vary a little in pace between venues, depending on the air conditioning in each building and how tightly the carpet is stretched. If it's tight it will run faster, and slower if there's a bit of slack, so it can vary in speed by one or two seconds. Wales is one of those venues where I always seem to play my best bowls. The first time I competed at Llanelli Indoor Bowls Centre in 1997, I felt really good playing there, got in a groove and won. The next time I played there in 2004, I drew inspiration from the previous win and had the belief that I could win it again. And that's what happened; I defended it again the following year. In fact, I put together something like 15 straight wins in the Welsh International Open in 1997, 2004 and 2005.

I've always believed that if I've won in a place before I can win there again, and I've won several singles tournaments a few times. Apart from winning the Welsh International Singles three times, I've also won the Bribie Island singles tournament three times, the Mount Isa singles three times and the Tweed Heads Golden Nugget three times. Knowing that I've already won there gives me confidence before I even start. For me, it's all about building momentum and having a positive attitude.

15

Selections and Apologies

During the weeks leading up to the 2006 Commonwealth Games, the squad stayed in Melbourne at a college opposite Princess Park in Parkville. The night before the announcement of the selection of the final team, we all gathered in the grassy downstairs courtyard. It was a night off our usual routine when everyone got together to enjoy the celebration of all the hard work that we'd put in over the previous twelve to 18 months of preparation for the Games. We had pizzas and drinks, and while we were enjoying each others' company, some of us were definitely feeling a bit edgy. There would have been 23 people in the group that night. Apart from the eight men and eight women vying for positions on the Commonwealth Games Team, there was also Cameron Curtis (the head coach), Ian Schuback (the assistant coach), Arnold O'Brien (the chairman of selectors), Damien Smeaton (the sports science advisor), Becky Dillon (the sports psychologist), Kim Littlejohn, (the high performance manager) and Shirley Blackwell (the chairperson of the ladies' selectors) present that night.

Throughout the night I kept thinking that I'd prepared

myself pretty well. I thought I'd either be playing singles or pairs, and if I wasn't playing singles that Steve Glasson would be selected for the coveted role.

The next morning, as we'd done each morning at the camp, we had a training session. At around 6.30am we gathered downstairs, went for a fast walk and a few stretches. After breakfast, a shower and packing our bags because we were leaving that day, we were told to gather in the courtyard. There, Kim Littlejohn advised us of the procedure for the team announcement. We were instructed that we were not to have any contact with family, friends or media, and that we had to hand our mobile phones to Damian Smeaton, who then proceeded to collect all phones from the squad members. We were told the phones would be returned after the team had been selected.

We were then called one by one to go to an upstairs room where Cameron Curtis and Arnold O'Brien were waiting to tell us of the selectors' decision. Each player was either told that they were in the team or they weren't in the team, and if selected they were told to go to a room down the hallway. Damian Smeaton called Barrie Lester's name first, and he ran into the room to be told, 'Congratulations, you've been selected for the Commonwealth Games, well done. When you leave the room, please make your way to the room down the hall.' Next was Billy Cornells, who was told the same thing, followed by Wayne Turly, Mark Casey (who skipped the men's triples) and Nathan Rice (who skipped the men's pairs).

At that stage the majority of the team members had gone in, and anyone else who followed had no contact with the people who'd been before — so I wasn't to know if Barrie or any of the other players who entered the room before me were in or out. I followed Nathan Rice and when I walked into the room I was told, 'Kelvin, you've been selected to play the singles at the Commonwealth Games.'

'Wow!' I thought to myself, 'That's pretty big.' I was over the moon to be given the honour of playing singles for Australia, and thought, 'Well, that means Steve Glasson must be playing in the pairs.'

I then exited the room, walked down the corridor about ten metres and went into the next room to join the rest of the Commonwealth Games men's team. Everyone else in that room was pretty excited because they'd all been selected, and I was the last one to enter. But then it hit us. There were six players in that room — six pretty happy people — but where was Steve Glasson?

Shane Globits, another member of the squad, was the next to front the selectors and after being informed he had missed out he was told to walk down to the end of the hallway. On his way, he heard us celebrating and poked his head around the door with disappointment in his face and said, 'Well done, guys.' He was then asked to continue down the hallway as he wasn't meant to catch up with us.

Steve Glasson was the last to be told that he hadn't made the Commonwealth Games team. One of the reasons they gave him was that he hadn't been committed enough to the high performance program that Bowls Australia had implemented over the previous year or two. At the time, his non-selection sent shockwaves through the place. I was very disappointed for him because we're great mates and Steve's one of the best players in the world on any given day. Obviously all the other guys were very excited that they'd been picked for the team, but at the same we time felt for Steve, and reflecting on how Steve must be feeling and how unlucky he was took the edge off our celebration.

Steve's form had been very good during the Commonwealth Games trials games and we were pretty evenly matched in the singles games we played against each other. From memory, I may have been just ahead on games wins but there was very little between us, which is why I would have been happy just being selected for the pairs and Steve for the singles. But it wasn't for lack of form that he missed selection but rather, according to the High Performance Team, his supposed lack of commitment to the programme.

A couple of years before the Commonwealth Games, Bowls Australia made some pretty big changes, implementing a high performance program with the aim of making players more professional and fitter than they had ever been before. When I was first selected into the Australian squad there really wasn't much of a program in place. We had several visits to the Institute of Sport in Canberra where we attended a few lectures and did a few fitness tests, just to see in general how fit we were. But apart from that, we played our competition bowls, and that was the extent of it.

However, once the high performance program was introduced, that all changed. Leading up to the Commonwealth Games, we all had to undergo a rigorous testing process that included skin fold measurements, a beat test and also rigorous stretching exercises. Each player was told what weight they had to achieve, what fitness level they had to reach and set an individual goal. So if you were carrying a little bit in excess weight, you may have been told to lose five or six kilos, and if you didn't lose those five or six kilos, that may have affected your Commonwealth Games selection. In fact, I was told that I should lose about four or five kilos. Guys such as Barrie Lester, who put in the extra hard yards and gave 120 percent on their fitness level, were looked upon favourably, even though their skill levels may not have been as high. With the Commonwealth Games tournament being an endurance event over ten days, a guy like Barrie would be almost guaranteed to be as fit and fresh on day ten as day one — a fact they took into account. What they were saying with Steve was that he hadn't shown that he was committed to the program, whether it was shedding a few kilos, giving up the smokes, or putting in at training. An important part of the program was to complete and submit a training diary each week. It included such details as how far you walked each week, how many bowls you put down each week, how much exercise you'd done — all those things you did to show a commitment to the sport and to bettering your performance. Some players were very conscientious in completing their diary, and others probably didn't take them as seriously as the coaching staff may have liked.

I know that some players didn't send in their diary every week, and that would have resulted in a cross beside their name. Certainly Steve's ability is second to none; he's one of the best players in the world. At the time, he was the defending world singles outdoor champion, and yet he couldn't make the top six in Australia for the Commonwealth Games team!

Once the team had been announced, we left the room and were told that we'd be making our way to the Darebin International Sports Centre where there would be a media conference with the Commonwealth Games Association, and the team would be made public. I went downstairs and saw Steve and said, 'Bad luck, mate, I don't know what's going on.' As you can imagine, Steve was gutted. I really felt for him, and I still say to this day that, even though it was one of the most successful Commonwealth Games teams ever in the history of bowls for Australia, Steve really should have been part of it.

Of course, the selectors and high performance staff would say they picked the best team and, to their credit, the results speak for themselves: three gold medals, two silver medals and a bronze, but with Steve Glasson in the side, I reckon it would've been four golds!

Steve not being part of the Commonwealth Games Team was one of the biggest disappointments of my career. We had come through the junior ranks together in Queensland, played in the Australian team together since 1995 and travelled the world together playing bowls. And then to have a Commonwealth Games in our home country, in Melbourne, a great sporting capital of the world, and for Steve not to be there — it just didn't seem right!

After the disappointment of the Manchester Games four years before, Bowls Australia was keen to leave no stone unturned in the quest for glory in Melbourne. A motivational coach came to speak to us and encouraged us all to think about how we were going to work together as a team to achieve the best possible results and to each write a Pledge to read to the other team members.

Here is my pledge:

Hello Team,

My first feelings of walking in with the Australian team at Manchester for my first games gave me bumps on the back of my neck, and I am sure that we as a team can now not wait for that excitement in Melbourne before starting our assault on winning gold for one another with this team!!!

I know since I have been a member of the Australian bowls team since 1995 there has never been this sort of build up as a team with such commitment to one another as we have now. I know I have had some great moments with other team members before but I will be prepared to, and will give 110 percent AT ALL TIMES. This is my commitment and I want to win!!! If you all have GOLD MEDALS by the time I play my final how good will that feeling be!!!

I believe we will be the best performed Australian team ever because of the team we have and the commitment we will all have for one another and the preparation process we have gone through. This is certainly the most preparation that I have ever done in any team I have been part of. I want to be part of this team, and help cheer us all so we can achieve and become successful Gold Medalists. Every second, every minute, every hour, every day is what it will take for our team to be great for nine days.

I WILL CONTRIBUTE TO MAKING OUR AUSSIE TEAM THE MOST FEARED AND RESPECTED TEAM IN THE WORLD, SO NO OTHER TEAM WILL EVER WANT TO PLAY US AGAIN BUT WATCH US IN AWE.

I WILL NEVER GIVE UP OR SURRENDER MY SPIRIT. I WILL ALWAYS ENJOY TEAM COMPANY, EACH INDIVIDUAL BRINGS SOMETHING UNIQUE AND WE WILL VALUE THIS TO HELP EACH OTHER SUCCEED.

I WILL ALWAYS DIG DEEPER WHEN MOST NEEDED. I WILL GIVE EVERY BOWL A CHANCE.

See you all next week.

Go AUSTRALIA!

The squad had practised at Darebin for eleven of the 14 weeks leading up to the Games and we arrived a week before the Games were due to start. We'd put in hours and hours of practice every day, and three days out we suggested that it would be great to have a free day. So, after a couple of hours practise in the morning, we all went to lunch together — the six ladies and the six men along with the high performance team of Cameron Curtis, Ian Schuback, Damian Smeaton, and the sports psychologist, Becky Dillon.

We had lunch at a restaurant beside the Yarra River and finished at about 2pm. We were told that the rest of the day was free, so we could do as we liked. The girls decided to go shopping then return to the Commonwealth Games village for dinner, whereas the men decided to have a few beers at one of the local restaurant-bars. We stayed there for an hour or so and then walked a couple of hundred yards to another bar and had a couple more beers. It was a nice bright blue sunny sky, a lovely day in Melbourne; being in the middle of March, the weather was hot and it was a great chill-out time amongst the boys. We had a few more beers as the sun went down.

At about 7pm, a couple of us received a text message from one of the high performance team asking, 'Where are you guys? Just wondering when you're coming back.' We thought, 'What's this? We've got a free day and they're sending us text messages already?' I think everyone just ignored it. Another 45 minutes went by and another text message came through along the lines of, 'Where the hell are you? Time to get back to the village. Get home now.' Obviously they'd known we were drinking. Four of the boys said, 'Well, I think we better head back. That message doesn't sound too good.' But I said, 'I'm sticking to my guns; a free day's a free day, I'm not going anywhere.' So Nathan Rice and I decided to stay while the other four headed back to the village. A little later, after the boys had returned, I get a message on my phone saying something like, 'Kelvin, get home right now, or else.' This was at about 9.30pm, so I said, 'Nathan, I think we'd better go,' and headed to the designated athletes' bus stop.

When we arrived back at the Commonwealth Games village, we went through security and walked to our unit. (The men's and ladies' teams were based in one building, a three-level apartment, with a couple of bedrooms on each floor). As we approached the front entrance of the apartment, there they were — Cameron Curtis, Kim Littlejohn and Damian Smeaton — waiting for us. They said, 'Okay, boys, we better have a chat. Let's go into the room.' The three of them sat on one bed, and Nathan and I sat on the opposite bed, looking at one another. I said to Nathan, 'Mate, don't say anything. Let them say what they wanna say, and I'll talk on your behalf. Just let me do all the talking, mate, just go along with whatever I say.'

So I said, 'Look, whatever you wanna say, guys, let's hear it.' They tore into us, saying they were pretty disappointed that we'd been out drinking. They agreed to give us a free day and we'd gone over the top with it and that we weren't committed to the rest of the team.

After they had said their piece, I gave it back to them. I told them that a free day on my terms is a free day. There was no curfew set. We'd had a great afternoon, been to a couple of bars, had several drinks, but we'd just been chilling out and hadn't done anything stupid. We'd just been a team of six guys enjoying one another's company and getting on like a house on fire. Then we get embarrassing text messages at 7pm and 8pm and 9pm demanding that we get home when we're having a free day. I got pretty fired up and basically told them that their attitude was uncalled for.

After I finished my outburst, I said, 'Hang on, I just need some time to think for a minute.' So I went outside and rang my mate Steve Glasson, and told him what had happened. I then said to Steve, 'I'm really pissed off at the way they're carrying on, and if I pull out of the Commonwealth Games tonight or in the morning, are you gonna take my place?' He replied,

'No way, I wouldn't take your place.' When he said that to me, I went back in and thought I'd give it to them a bit more, thinking that, seeing as the Commonwealth Games starts in only a few days, I've got them by the balls. They're not going to have a singles player, so I'll give them a bit more. So I went back in and said, 'I'm absolutely embarrassed, not just for myself but for the rest of the team members, that you've treated us like kindergarten kids. We're grown adults, equal to you. We give 110 percent commitment and have done everything you've wanted us to do. We ask for a free day, we get a free day, then you ask us to be home by eight o'clock.' Then, caught up in my bravado, I dropped a bombshell and said, 'I'm gonna pull out of the Commonwealth Games tomorrow morning at nine o'clock unless I receive an apology from each of you, and I'm going straight to Perry Crosthwaite, the CEO of the Commonwealth Games Association' — who I'd met before at the Manchester Commonwealth Games — 'to tell him exactly what has happened.' This sent shockwaves through the place because what I didn't realise was that I was talking at the top of my voice and the rest of the ladies' and men's teams had their heads around the corner listening to the conversation taking place, and they just couldn't believe their ears. When we went to bed, things were still pretty tense.

I was rooming with Barrie Lester and Nathan Rice and I said to them at 8.30am the next morning, 'I'm serious about this. If I don't receive an apology, I'm out of here.' Barrie and Nathan were shitting themselves, saying, 'You can't do this, Kelvin.' I just replied, 'Nah, mate, I'm doing it. They can't treat us like kids. We gotta stick up for ourselves.' Then, at about quarter to nine, Damien Smeaton knocked on the door. 'Kelvin, you know, I'm sorry about last night. It probably was a little bit over the top and it shouldn't have happened. Let's just let it all go by now.'

'Yeah, no worries, apology accepted.'

Then ten minutes later, at about three minutes to nine, head coach Cameron Curtis knocked on the door, and said, 'About last night, we got a bit hot, probably had to get it out of our system. I apologise for anything that was said, I take it all back. Let's not worry about it now.'

'Yep, no worries, apology accepted.'

When he left, I said to Nathan, 'That's bloody good of those two to apologise, but if Kim doesn't come by, I'm out of here.'

At one minute to, Kim knocks on the door — the door's open but he sort of just stands there and does a little tap because I'm right at the doorway.

'Kelvin, about last night, I'm really sorry.' He was nearly crying; it was hurting him so much that he had to apologise.

'Yeah, no worries,' I said. 'Apology accepted, no problems.'

We then all got on the bus at 10am for training at the Darebin Sport Centre. We had a scheduled practice at 10.30am but it just wasn't the same — no one was talking. Everyone was still in shock from the night before; the team harmony was shot to pieces because the coaches weren't happy, the players weren't happy with what had happened, and you could feel the tension in the air. After practice, we got back on the bus, then off the bus and straight into the Games village dining hall for lunch. I don't think the coaches came in, or if they did they sat on a different table. I said, 'Listen guys, about last night, obviously there's tension and I think we've got to get it out of our system. Let's get together and thrash it out. How about we arrange a meeting after lunch where we get together with the high performance team and the coaches, get in a circle, and if anybody's got anything they wanna say about the last week — about training, about practising, or who they're rooming with, or any problems at all — let's get it off our chests.'

The ladies' captain, Karen Murphy, and Wayne Turly, the men's captain, arranged the meeting, saying that the players wanted to meet with the high performance team to talk about what had happened the previous night and any issues that may affect the team, because we're playing bowls for Australia in two days.

So we all sat in chairs in a circle and thrashed it out and reaffirmed our pledges to each other. Every single member had their say, including the coaches, and we bitched and whinged and everyone got it out of their systems. And you wouldn't believe it, but there was never a happier team or a happier time than the next ten days. Everyone got on like a million dollars and everyone supported each other. When we were playing, the girls watched and when the girls were playing, the men watched. I think a large part of our success was that we were all committed to one another and everyone wanted to win. Not everyone could win, but the Games were an absolute 'belter'. We became the most successful Australian bowls team ever.

16

The Commonwealth Games

The Commonwealth Games were fantastic. To start with, having the opportunity to walk out on the MCG in front of a huge crowd was electric, something I'll never forget.

I had a kind schedule that allowed me to sleep in the day after the opening ceremony, whereas the triples had a 10am start. The men's singles didn't start for five days, so I could support the men's and ladies' triples and pairs before I played. This provided an opportunity to talk to my team members and discuss the conditions on particular greens and particular rinks, so I could gather information and see if conditions had changed since our practice sessions.

After weeks of intensive practice on all four greens at the Darebin Sports Centre leading up to the Games, we knew each green and each rink like the backs of our hands. We had taken notes on how each rink was playing. They varied not only between each other, but the forehand on one rink might be bendier than the backhand or there might have been a little hill on the roadside of one of the rinks. We also adjusted to the slowness of the greens — they were slow by Australian standards, paced at around eleven or twelve seconds — and the maximum size of the greens, which measured 40 metres ditch to ditch.

All this practice and knowledge gave us a huge advantage over the other countries, who had rocked in only a week or so before the Games started. They had to get over the trip from the UK, or wherever they were from, and had limited practice time as all the countries had to be allocated practice time slots.

By the time my first round came, I was ready to play. I wouldn't say I was nervous; it was more a case of being psyched to get started because I'd seen my other team members playing really well and making the finals, so it gave me a buzz to perform well myself.

First up I played Douw Calitz from Namibia who I'd never seen before, let alone played. I got off to a flier with a convincing win and my tournament was up and running.

The second round the next day started after lunch, which suited me fine. It gave me time to wander down to the games village at about 11.30 in the morning, chill out and have a light snack. I like to have something to eat an hour or two before I play, and don't like getting to the venue too early. I usually arrive about half an hour before playing, just enough time to change, polish my bowls and focus on the two end roll-up which gives me vital information about the conditions on the rink. I played Malaysia's Mohd Affendy Tan Abdullah, and I knew it was going to be a pretty tough match. I continued my good form to easily win the first set, but then lost the second and managed to win the match on a tiebreak.

I had the next day off due to the ladies' and men's triples

finals being played, so it was a chance for me watch them win medals. That's when the Games started to get really exciting. The ladies won silver in the triples in the afternoon, and then the men's triples finals kicked off at about quarter to seven that night. It was an absolute cracker of a game, with a great crowd and atmosphere to match. To watch the men win gold was an absolute inspiration for me and I was fired up to make the singles final.

The boys had a huge night of celebration and I don't think they went to sleep for 24 hours. Unfortunately I couldn't join them because I was scheduled to play the next day at 1pm. I had a bit of a hiccup in this game, being beaten by Peter Juni of Papua New Guinea. One of the reasons I went down in this match, suffering my only loss of the tournament, was that I experimented with a different set of bowls. I felt that the greens were starting to run a little bit quicker, which I put down to the fact that Darebin hadn't had many scheduled matches in the few months that we'd trained there leading up to the Games (after several days of continuous competition, the greens flatten out, start to run a second quicker and turn a bit more).

In the lead-up trials and practice for the Games, I used my Taylor Ace bowls, which are suited to slow greens, and then switched to a set of Vectors for the first rounds of the tournament. When the greens seemed to be playing a bit quicker, I started having second thoughts and changed to an old set of Taylor Redlines, which are a little narrower than the newer sets, and draw a fair bit less than the Vectors. Unfortunately, this decision backfired on me and I found it hard to get around some of the shorter bowls. It probably cost me a lot in that match. I thought I played reasonably well, but ended up losing to Juni in a tiebreak.

The other reason I lost this match was because Peter Juni had an absolute blinder. He walked on water that day and played like a champion. I've got to give the guy credit; he out-played me and deserved to win. I was pretty disappointed after the game because I felt that not only had I let myself down, but also the capacity crowd that was willing me on. Australia probably shouldn't lose to Papua New Guinea because they just haven't got the experience and the quality that we have in Australia, so it was a real wake-up call for me. But it was still early in the tournament and I had to put the loss out of mind. I decided that I would return to using the Vector bowls for the rest of the tournament.

In my next round I was up against Martin McHugh, one of Ireland's top players. I knew this was going to be a tough battle, and in one of my best games of the tournament I won in straight sets in what was actually a pretty tight game. I was relieved to have my Games campaign back on track.

At this stage of the tournament we were down to the knockout stage with the top eight qualifiers. This was crunch time and I was all business when I played a rock-solid game to knock out Nkole Edward Kasonde of Zambia in a high-quality match. Knowing that I was able to take my game to the next level when the pressure was on gave me confidence going into the semi-finals the next day.

I had a good sleep that night knowing I had a pretty good chance of getting a medal. But I wasn't going to be happy with a bronze or silver; I was set on the gold. I had watched the ladies' pairs, Karen Murphy and Lynsey Armitage, win the gold medal and seen them stand on the dais with gold medals around their necks and the national anthem playing, and this spurred me on. Nothing short of standing on the top pedestal with gold around my neck and the anthem playing was going to satisfy me.

The next morning I was in the semi-final against England's Stephen Farish, who had been one of the best outdoor players in England over the past five years. He had been the English national champion a couple of times and I knew this was going to be a really hard-fought game, and it was. I got away to a slow start and was behind in the first set but fought my way back with a two on the last end to make it a draw and keep my hopes alive. The second set was tight all the way, and from 5–5 I battled my way to being a shot up going into the last end of the second set and I managed to pick up one to secure the win. The match was so close that we could have easily tied the two sets, but because I drew the first set and won the second, I was through to the final. That was an absolute dream and just blew me away. Whatever happened now was a good result, but I knew there was never going to be another chance in my lifetime to be playing for a gold medal in front of my home crowd in Melbourne.

With the men's singles final taking place the next night at 7pm, there was about 30 hours of anticipation, waiting and hopefully sleep to get through. The thought of the huge crowd and the excitement of being in the gold medal game kept me awake most of the night and I knew I had to relax before the match. So the next morning I organised a day pass for my wife, Karen, and the kids to visit the Games village to take my mind away from the game. We spent a few hours together strolling around and having lunch in the athletes' food hall. After they left in the mid-afternoon, I just chilled out for a few hours by myself, watched a bit of TV, and tried to relax as if it were just another day.

I changed my tactics a bit once I reached the quarter-finals and went back to playing a medium three-quarter length as the greens became a little bit quicker. On the night of the final, the green was running at about 13 seconds, the quickest for the whole tournament. There had been so much bowls played on the greens that they'd worn down a bit, and the greens keepers would have rolled them before the final that night, giving them even more pace. So I didn't think that there was any real advantage to play ditch-to-ditch and felt that I could get more rhythm playing a medium length. Once it got to the nitty-gritty of the final eight players, there was not really going be a great advantage just playing ditch-to-ditch because they could all probably play ditch-to-ditch. I knew that Robert Weale and Stephen Farish both played a lot of long ends, so I decided to revert to playing three-quarter lengths that I was more used to.

I arrived at the venue about an hour before I was set to play. It was a perfect night; there wasn't a breath of wind or a cloud in the sky, and I was pretty excited as I got off the bus and walked through the front gates. There were a few well-wishers to meet me at the gates, saying, 'All the best!', 'Good luck!' and, 'Aussie, Aussie, Aussie!' Also waiting to greet me were my wife Karen, my kids Kirk and Ky, my parents, my sister Katrina and my aunty Delma, which helped put me in a positive frame of mind. As I walked out of the glass doors and onto the green where the finals were to be held, I saw the large grandstand of spectators eagerly waiting an hour before the game. The lights were already on even though it was still light, and it was just one of those nights when I couldn't have wished for better conditions. I felt as though I was meant to be there and that my whole life had been destined towards this match. I'd played Robert Weale many times in the UK on indoor surfaces, and he's a good friend of mine, but I had never had the opportunity to play him in Australia on an outdoor green. So we were probably on an equal playing field. Robert had come through the tournament in pretty good form as well, so I was really looking forward to the match.

About half an hour before the game I put the Australian stickers on my bowls, polished them and set them up next to the match rink. Before I knew it, Robert and I were being introduced onto the green to a huge roar and cheers of 'Aussie, Aussie, Aussie!'. I actually felt a bit for Robert who not only had to contend with me but also with the home-country crowd. Having the crowd support was an advantage for me, as I knew I'd get loud applause whenever I got anything close, whereas if he wasn't going so well, it could affect him mentally, knowing that he'd have to have a resting toucher to get a clap.

I dropped four shots in three ends at the start of the first set but I didn't let any doubt creep into my mind. The crowd kept me 'up' and were doing their best to inspire a turnaround and with their support I started to fight my way back. It was a really tight game in the first set with only eleven shots scored in the first nine ends, but I managed to win the it 7–4. When the announcement was made, 'First set 7–4 to Kerkow', the crowd went berko, which probably spooked me a little as I couldn't help thinking to myself, 'I've only got to win this set now and I've got the gold medal.' Over the years, I've learnt that when you think you've won the game before it's over, it's when you lose the game. I'd learnt from playing hundreds and hundreds of singles games throughout my career that whenever I'm playing a guy who was in front of me and he only needed one or two to win, and I'm six or seven or even ten shots behind, I'd think that was my chance to make a comeback. Because as soon as someone thinks 'I've won this game,' or 'I think I'm gonna beat ya,' it mentally affects their game and that's when they get nervous and you can clean 'em up.

So I tried to start the second set as if it were the first, to switch off and start again. I'm not exactly sure what went wrong, but I guess Robert grew an extra leg and took his game up a notch. He got a good start and jumped away to a 4–1 break in the second set. I couldn't get back into the set and he went on to win it 9–2. The crowd was cheering louder than ever to get me up, but I was now on the back foot and knew that at one set each in the best of three ends tiebreak it could go either way.

I called 'heads' and won the toss, and the option to keep or give the mat away. I made my way to Cameron Curtis, the head coach who was sitting on a chair at the edge of the green. He stood up and I asked him, 'Mate, what do you think I should do?' But really I was just trying to slow the game down and take a breather, because I knew that when I returned to the mat it was going to be game on. Cameron suggested I take the mat but I backed my own hunch and decided to give it away and have the last bowl.

I drew an early shot and then played my third bowl around the back for safety. Now the pressure was on Weale's last bowl. He needed to draw inside my shot-bowl or the gold was mine. I held my breath as he delivered, joined by the 2000-strong crowd in silent prayer. The bowl looked good out of the hand and I started to have that sinking feeling. Then, again in those last few metres, it began to pull up, but not before running into my bowl, turning it a little closer to the jack.

I won!

My Australian team-mates ran onto the green and swamped me. Pure elation took over and I ripped off my shirt as I ran the length of the green, waving it above my head.

This was not something that I had consciously planned to do, but in the excitement of the moment I fulfilled a promise made at a Grand Prix event at Helensvale in 2005, when my partner Brett Duprez and I lost the doubles final to Nathan Rice and Barry Lester. Barry is a pretty fit bloke and he lifted his shirt to show off his six-pack to me. It was his first major win, so I didn't begrudge him, but when I shook his hand I told him that if I won the Commonwealth Games I would take my shirt off and millions would see it.

I had forgotten all about the pledge until that night at Darebin. In the spur of the moment, off came the shirt. As I said, I don't think it was conscious; I was just caught up in the joy of the victory.

I guess it made me something of an instant celebrity. Lawn bowlers are not renowned as the most demonstrative of sportspeople, but hey, I'd come a long way and I was sure as hell going to enjoy it.

After the Gold

Winning the gold medal for Australia was a dream come true for me. It made all the pain, the long hours of practice and the time away from home worthwhile. It also gave me added confidence in my ability when facing up to new challenges, both on the World Tour and at home, in playing the world's best.

David Gourlay has probably been the best indoor player in the world over the last ten years. Although Scottish, David has played a lot of his bowls in Australia, but is at his most consistent best on the carpet in the UK. He was rated the number one or two bowler on the World Tour in the four years leading up to my finals clash with him in the 2006 Scottish International Open.

I was rated nine in the world at the time and was keyed up for the match. I burst out of the blocks to take a commanding lead and went on to win in straight sets, 11–5, 13–3. David had lost a few of his recent World Bowls Tour finals, and I think that may have been playing on his mind, so I wanted to put him under pressure from the first end. After the match,

Gourlay stated: 'He played really well and put me under so much pressure with his first bowls. The first bowl is key, and once your opponent's on a roll it's so difficult … He just never missed.' I was quoted in the press as saying that it was a 'fairy tale' and that 'there was no way I could have imagined doing this against a player like David'.

That match probably goes to show that any one of the top 16 players in the World Bowls Tour could beat any of the others on any given day. There isn't really a great deal of difference, although the top seeds have been a little more consistent. In particular, I find David Gourlay, Alex Marshall, Greg Harlow and Paul Foster to be the four toughest guys to play against. Alex Marshall is very versatile, being equally as good outdoors as he is indoors whereas David Gourlay and Greg Harlow are real indoor specialists. I'm pretty competitive in both and I've beaten all the top-ranked bowlers and they've also beaten me. I don't think there's anyone in particular that I dominate or that dominates me, and there're no real grudges between anyone.

◎   ◎   ◎

In September 2006 I was invited as part of an Australian team to a tournament in South Africa called the Tri-Nations. It was held at the Emperor's Palace Casino in Johannesburg, and included South Africa, Australia and the UK.

It is one of the more enjoyable and social tournaments I have ever played in. A good friend of mine, Steve Boylan, who recently passed away, was the bowls director and the driving force behind staging the tournament. Steve did a great job in attracting the best bowlers in the world, including Robert Weale, David Gourlay, Greg Harlow and Amy Monkhouse for the British Lions. Representing South Africa were Gerry Baker, who'd been a champion singles player for over ten years; Wayne Perry, who was the new face of bowls in South Africa; and Lorna Trigwell, probably the best South African lady bowler ever. There also was Donny Piketh, a South African Commonwealth Games gold medallist.. My team-mates were Steve Glasson, Karen Murphy and Wayne Turly.

The Casino and accommodation was unbelievably huge and lavish, so big that there is a rollercoaster inside! Another memorable feature of the place was that the stubbies were only $1! Everything was set up for the perfect tournament; however, the locals kept cautioning us about one thing: the sheilas. We were warned to always hang on to our drinks and never leave them on the bar, because in the past, sheilas had dropped pills in guys' drinks without them being aware. If you were drugged, you could become totally disoriented and even collapse, and before you know it, your wallet, phone and any other valuables would be gone. Also, as you come into the casino, you had to walk through a metal detector just like at the airport, and at the end of that they had a 'gun deposit' box, so people coming in had to pull out their guns and put them in. This all happened just outside the bar we were drinking at, which made the place a little scary.

I had been at the bar having a few drinks with Greg Harlow, who's a solid guy who can hold his grog, along with my team-mates Steven Glasson and Wayne Turly. We had a few drinks and then a flutter at the tables with some of the other players. It was about 11pm when I spoke to Greg at a table before having a last drink at the bar and heading back on the long trek of about 400 metres to my room.

The next thing, I see Greg coming towards me. The hallway was about four metres wide and he was staggering from one wall to another; he could hardly walk. I asked him, 'Mate, are you alright? What happened?' But he was slurring his words and I couldn't make out what he was saying. He was off his face and didn't have a clue where he was. So I walked him to his room, got his key from his pocket, let him in and he crashed on the bed. The next morning, we all got up for breakfast as normal looking forward to starting the tournament. But there was no sign of Greg and we had to call a doctor. He was as sick as a dog and had to spend the next 48 hours in bed.

The Brits had to replace Greg at short notice, but spearheaded by an inspirational performance by Gourlay, they won the right to play us for the title. But without Greg they weren't as competitive and we triumphed. The St John's Park Bowling Club in Sydney donated the new trophy, aptly named the Steve Boylan Cup after the event's originator (who was unable to attend the event due to illness), and the prize money was a healthy $12,000 for the winning team, so $3000 each. However, rather than receiving a cheque, we were paid in $100 casino chips, which was a first for all of us. So we each had to go to a casino cashier to cash in the chips. Karen Murphy thought she was being watched and then followed when she cashed hers, so she ended up running through the casino with a bag full of money!

Up until 2009, Merv and I had both won the World Indoor

pairs two times: once together and once with other partners. Merv won with Tony Allcock the year after I won with Ian Schuback in 1998. We also lost the final together in 2007 against David Gourlay and Billy Jackson. In 2009 we had an opportunity to avenge that defeat when we found ourselves up against Gourlay and Jackson again.

Merv and I had not conceded a set during the entire week and were keen to carry that form into the final. We jumped to a 5–0 lead on the back of Merv's impeccable leading, before Jackson and Gourlay started to apply some pressure. But we held on to win the first set (of eleven ends) by a two-shot margin. Jackson and Gourlay took the upper hand in the second set, and clung to an 8–7 margin going into the final end. With Merv holding a single shot advantage to tie the set, I put down a 'blocker' with my last bowl, which left Gourlay almost no chance of reclaiming the lead. We both pumped the air when Gourlay's final delivery failed to dislodge our shot bowl.

It was a sweet victory, and we made up for my early departure in 2005 and really partied. At the height of the celebration, I remember emptying a full bottle of champagne over my Australian supporters at about 2am. It cost me £40 and it was all gone in about five seconds! I shook it up and sprayed it every where; I remember the bubbles running down the window. Obviously, I was a very sick puppy the next day, but very happy. It was a good win. I obviously couldn't have done it without Merv, who is one of the best players I've ever had the privilege to compete with and I rank him as one of the best in the world — and certainly the best lead I've ever seen.

Holding high my Welsh International trophy after my win in 2004.

Australian coach, Robbie Dobbins congratulates me on winning the gold medal in the singles at the Asia Pacific Games, Dunedin 1995.

With my team mates at South Tweed Bowling Club: Premier League winner, 2000.

Commonwealth Games Gold Medal ceremony with Robert Weale of Wales on my left and the Bronze Medallist, Ryan Bester on my right.

The Australian World Bowls team, 2004, Ayre, Scotland
(L-R) Brett Duprez, myself, Steve Glasson, Robbie Dobbins (Manager), Michael Wilks, Kevin Walsh.

The opening ceremony of the 2004 World Championships.

Sweeping water off the greens before the start of play in the
2004 World Championships.

Calling the shot at the 2004 World Championships in Scotland.

Victory in the Scottish International Open, 2006
Nigel Oldfield, CEO of the World Bowls Tour at left and the Managing Director
of the major sponsor, Great British Mobility Group.

Merv King and I, World Indoor Pairs
Champions, 2009.

At home with Karen, Ky and Kirk.

My three cherished Golden Nuggets... and I'm shooting for my fourth.

South Tweed Division 1 team, 2009.

With Mum and Dad, who made it all possible.

Moving On

After much soul-searching and discussion with my family, I submitted my resignation to Bowls Australia at the Queensland Open in July 2008, advising them that I would be unavailable to represent Australia in future games. The main reason was that I'd been representing my country for 13 years since 1995 and during that time I had been away from my family for long periods of time. Playing at the elite level involves so much time these days, especially with the introduction of the high performance programme into the sport. Then there's the financial side. The time devoted to training and practising and spending time overseas, whether it be for Commonwealth or World Bowls commitments, provided too little return financially for my growing family.

I was approaching 40 and starting to feel that my best days of competitive bowls were behind me. My fitness level wasn't as good as it was three years before, and my passion for the game was probably not as great as it was five years before. I still really enjoy it competitively; I love the game to death, but at the end of the day I had to come to terms with getting older and getting the balance right between bowls and family.

I recently hurt my right foot while bowling, and a specialist confirmed that I had a light fracture in my right ankle. He told me it was due to a large build-up of arthritis in my right foot since the operation in my teenage years. He cautioned that this could deteriorate over the coming years, and by the time I reach 50 I may even struggle to walk. So, I guess this has also played on my mind a little.

Looking back, I probably didn't get to spend enough time with my eldest son Kirk, so it's important that I can be involved in the life of Ky, my youngest son — to be able to go to his football training and spend a couple of late afternoons kicking a football around with him.

When an opportunity arose to come on board and work on a full-time basis with BCIB (Bowling Club Insurance Brokers), I felt that the timing was right to move on in my career. BCIB had been a past sponsor of mine and I had done some promotional work for them, so when they gave me the opportunity to learn the trade and become a qualified insurance broker (insuring bowling clubs across Australia), it seemed like a natural progression and too good an opportunity to turn down, especially as there was no guarantee I would have the opportunity again.

I'd been playing bowls on a full-time basis over the past 15 years, and this was a new road for me, the start of the rest of my life. The new role still allows me to play in the major tournaments, not just across Australia but around the world, including the World Indoor Championships in the UK.

An aspect of my new job that I really enjoy is being able

to get out and mix and talk to the general public in bowling clubs across Australia. As a past Australian player I have been warmly welcomed by club presidents and committees to clubs and I am happy to be representing an insurance product that helps support their club. But on top of that, it gives me an opportunity to put something back into the sport that has been so good to me. If they have a special club anniversary, such as a 50th or a 100th, or other special occasion, I'm in a position where I can contribute my services to the club, to help them have a great day.

I sent my resignation to Neil Dalrymple, the CEO of Bowls Australia, and I also sent copies to the high performance manager, Kim Littlejohn, and the head coach, Cameron Curtis. At the time, the Queensland Open was taking place at Cleveland Bowling Club in Brisbane, and the resignation was sent mid-afternoon via email. I think they were very disappointed with my decision, especially as I'd made it without any discussion and it took them by surprise. However, it was not a decision I made lightly, and came after several months of deliberation and talking with my family.

I am still keen to play bowls on a competitive level and compete in the World Indoor championships in the UK in the years to come as well as play pennant on a more consistent basis at my own club, South Tweed. I have missed a lot of pennant games at South Tweed over the last ten years, and I look forward to giving much more value to my club in the future and seeing the rising stars from my club come through for the future.

I owe a lot to South Tweed. They were my full-time employer for ten years until November 2008 and they supported me and my family the entire time I was away playing for Australia at events such as the World Indoor tournaments in the UK. They paid me a salary week in, week out, and there was a job at the club waiting for me when I returned. Being the club's Bowls Promotions Officer and the coach of up-and-coming juniors and members of the club, I was also fortunate to learn aspects of the hospitality industry. It's fair to say that a major part of my success over the last ten years has been due to the great support of my South Tweed Sports Club, including the members, the management and the board.

On the night of my Commonwealth Games win in 2006, most of the 500 members were packed into the club, watching the match on the big screen. My sister Bronwyn and her husband were there that night with the club manager, Gordon Rhodes, who said, 'We've got to watch and cheer Kelvin on.' A couple of members from the club even made the trip to Melbourne to watch me play and celebrate the win. When I returned, the South Tweed Bowls Club put on a 'welcome back' night for me. Again, the clubhouse was absolutely packed and when I walked in I was met at the front door by board members and club members, all wanting to see me with the gold medal around my neck.

The day after I made my decision to resign from the National squad, I said to Karen, 'If I'm going to win anything this year, I want it to be the Golden Nugget.'

In the first round of the 2008 Golden Nugget I was up against the Queensland Open runner-up, Mark Casey, who had been the in-form player of the previous few months. My battle with Mark was like a final. There was really nothing in it and I just got over the line 25–23. This gave me a good base for the tournament and on the way to the final I had wins over the 2007 runner-up, Matthew Pietersen, Kiwi star Ali Forsyth, and my former Aussie team-mate Nathan Rice.

I completed my quest with a 25–7 victory over New Zealand's dual world champion Gary Lawson in the final. I made a little bit of history by becoming the first male bowler to win three Golden Nugget crowns.

It was fitting that my mate Steve Glasson won the 2009 Golden Nugget to equal my three-time record. But look out, Steve, I'm gunning for a fourth!

Kelvin's Coaching Clinic

The Big C's

Over the years, I have been asked to give coaching advice and to answer a wide variety of questions by bowlers about every conceivable aspect of the game. In this section of the book I'm going to pass on some of the best advice that I have received in my career and some of the lessons I've learnt. I'm also going to give you some of the questions and answers from a clinic I have been conducting on the internet in recent years.

I hope that you will find something in my coaching clinic that will help you improve your game.

When I first started out, a fine coach emphasised the importance of the Big C's in bowls:

CONCENTRATION and **CORRECTION** gives **CONSISTENCY**.

COMPATIBILITY and **COMMITMENT** makes **CHAMPIONS**.

Please do me a favour. If you haven't taken a few steps to becoming a little health-conscious, try and do so, as it will help with your mental alertness and give you that extra confidence on the green!

There are so many bowlers, of different skill levels, who have proved that being a bit healthier and fitter has improved their bowling performance. It's very hard to play well when you are feeling uncomfortable through lack of fitness, and when you get tired, your concentration can easily wane.

Your Equipment

To kick off this clinic, here are some tips on what equipment you should have and what I personally look for in bowls gear. Let's start with some basic stuff.

Bowls Grippo/Wax – which one?

There are many brands and types of waxes available.

Personally, I do not use grippo of any kind, although very occasionally I will use the 'Champion' spray (from South Africa) and I will use this only after I have played on a wet day. The day after playing on a wet surface, my bowls get that glossy, dry sort of feel, and this is when I spray my bowls with this wax. I am probably one of a minority who do not use wax regularly on my bowls. I know many bowlers prefer to have that tacky feel but I feel comfortable without the wax. However, you may have a different body makeup to me. Maybe your hands sweat a lot or maybe they always have that very dry feel about them, in which case you may opt for the wax.

Make time to try a sample of all the waxes until you find one that suits you best. I know some bowlers who have two types: one for wet conditions and one for dry conditions.

Bowls Cloth

Again, I am different from most. I think 95 percent of bowlers use a bowls cloth, but I do not use a bowls cloth or even a chamois. Many bowlers are amazed that I don't even wipe my bowls clean during wet conditions when the bowl collects grit and grass. I find that the bowl has more grip with the dirt on the bowl (not clumps of dirt, of course). The bowl just feels better to me and I find that you can't get the bowl completely dry using a bowls cloth anyway.

The only time I would use a bowls cloth is when I play a very early morning game and there is some dew on the grass, which my bowl picks up. I suggest you try one of the chamois cloths that are now available.

Chalk or 'Toucha' Spray?

I know that many bowlers prefer 'toucha' spray because it is the least likely to move a bowl when marking it as a toucher, but I still prefer chalk.

I have found that chalk stays on the bowl in all conditions whereas the spray sometimes has problems.

To explain this further, I have a pretty quick drive and I

remember on one occasion that my opponent had a jack high toucher. I drove his bowl into the ditch and the 'toucha' spray that was used to mark the bowl was wiped off with the action of the bowl spinning in the ditch. I guess this is a pretty rare occurrence and at the end of the day it comes down to your personal preference.

Bowls Measures

A measure is an essential item for every bowler. The type of measure doesn't really matter as long as you have one that works properly. I have seen some pretty horrendous tapes with kinks. The good measures are expensive but they are definitely worth the money.

The measure is probably the most borrowed item amongst bowlers and also the one that goes missing the most often so take care of your own!

Rule Book

An up-to-date rule book is another 'must have' for all bowlers.

Make sure you take time to read the book several times — not during a game though. Makes good toilet reading … after you've read this book, of course!

It is so important to understand the rules of the game, particularly when you are in a tight contest against a crafty opponent. New rules are being introduced almost every year, so check with the umpires at your club — now!

A new rule that will work to my advantage is 'the foot over the mat at time of delivery'. It states that part of the foot must be on or over the mat at time of delivery whereas previously the whole foot had to be on or over the mat. In my opinion this is not a good rule as it is open to some abuse, but it's great for my forehand drive as I can get a tighter line with part of my foot off the mat.

Another new rule is the minimum length of jack roll from 21 metres to 23 metres. This doesn't worry me as I already play to the 23 metre rule in international competitions.

The Right Bowls for You

The most important aspect of your armoury is the bowls you decide to use. The most asked question put to top bowlers these days is which bowls they are using, and this is usually followed by the further question, 'Why?'

I must tell you that I am sponsored by the Taylor Bowls organisation, and use their products exclusively. I use Redline Taylor Bowls as I prefer a bowl that holds a nice banana-shape line to the jack — and the Redline does exactly that. They are not the narrowest bowls going around; I have found it very hard to use the narrower bowls as they are prone to follow blemishes in greens and are very tricky in windy conditions.

On greens that are very slow or holding, particularly in the UK, and also on couch grass greens, I may use Vector or Pinnacle bowls.

However, depending on where you live and what type of greens you play most of your bowls on, the best bowl for you is an entirely personal choice. Above all, the bowls you select *must* feel good in your hand, otherwise you will never be comfortable with them.

Please work with your coach when you select a new set of bowls. The most important thing to watch is the size of the bowl. Make sure it is not too big, or you may find that you drop the bowl when you deliver.

Don't think for a minute that I intend to get into an argument about which manufacturer makes the best set of bowls. However, because it is such a hot topic, I do wish to advise bowlers as to the type of bowl best suited to their playing conditions.

There are so many different bowls on the market today. Anyone trying to sort through the different types can become completely confused and eventually buy and sell two or three sets before they get the set that suits them, their greens and weather conditions.

I reckon I have tried almost all of the current bowl models and I'm familiar with virtually every type of bowling green there is, so you have to trust me on this issue.

You can't just look at your own club green and say you want a set suited to it. Maybe if you are a social bowler and play 98 percent of your bowls at home then your choice is much simpler. But if you are, for instance, a pennant player, then you are obliged to look at the general greens conditions in your area.

For instance, if you live in a coastal area you should think about weather conditions, in particular the effect wind will have on your bowl. Likewise, with so many synthetic greens around these days — some running at a very fast pace — it is difficult to adjust if you also have slow to ultra-slow grass greens to contend with. I'd suggest, however, that the majority of bowlers would not subscribe to this theory, believing they can make the necessary adjustment within their own deliveries.

Firstly, I have to admit to a couple of personal dislikes, and experience tells me that I have the backing of almost all top bowlers who, by their selection of bowls, agree with me.

They are:

- Bowls with a 'hockey stick' bend. Whilst they are reasonable on the draw playing on slow greens, the same can't be said for weighted shots. The weight is absolutely critical and there is no margin for error, particularly if the wind is blowing. On faster greens, the finishing trajectory is far too severe.

- Ultra-narrow drawing bowls. They are (a) too difficult to judge weight, (b) will hold out if you don't deliver the bowl precisely on the running surface, and (c) are adversely affected by wind.

My suggestions:

- I am absolutely adamant that the most important aspect of your selection is to select the bowl with the most regular arc, all the way from the mat to the jack. Any variations to this type of bowl will cause difficulties in windy conditions and also make weighted shots harder to achieve because, like the hockey stick bend bowls, weight is just too critical.

- Use a wide drawing bowl if you play most of your bowls on greens running 12 to 14 seconds.

- Choose the narrower drawing, regular arc-type bowl when playing predominantly on faster surfaces, particularly tiff dwarf grass and synthetics.

- Having made your selection carefully, you must practice purposefully and strive to achieve a natural delivery technique to become a consistent bowler.

Shoes

Please put some thought into the shoe you select. There is nothing more annoying than sore feet after the second game of the day or when you come in for the break in Pennant. Sore feet sidetrack you from the task at hand, so make sure your shoes are comfortable.

Choose carefully because if you are a regular bowler this shoe will be the most worn in your shoe closet.

The Basics

Preparation for Delivery of Jack

With the rule changes in international and local competition, the privilege of rolling of the jack by the lead is entirely up to the skip of the winning end. The skip has the option of handing the mat and jack to the opposition, or keeping the mat and having his lead roll the jack. In singles, the winner of the last end has the option to roll the jack or hand it to his opponent.

The Mat: What Would You Do?

You hear many skips saying, 'Keep the mat so that we can determine the length.' You also hear skips saying, 'Hand the mat over. I want the last bowl.'

I normally hand the mat to my opponent so that I have the last bowl because I believe that I can change my situation in an end with my last bowl. If I don't have last bowl, I have to hope my opposition doesn't change the head.

If you remember my final in the Commonwealth Games, I checked with Cameron Curtis what I should do with the mat and jack as I had won the end before the tie-break. As it turned out, I handed the mat to my opposition and this was the best move I have made in my life of bowls. It gave me the opportunity to place more pressure on my opposition as I had last bowl.

The rest is now history. I have the gold medal, and it still feels great!

There are still competitions in which the jack must be rolled by the winner of the last end. In these cases, in a team game I would talk to my team and get a consensus of opinion on what length to roll the jack.

If my opposition is struggling with short ends I will bring the mat right up and have the lead roll to the 'T'. The minimum length is now 23 metres, so I would give the lead a one-metre leeway; therefore, from 24 metres down to 23 metres is perfect. You can sometimes see the body language of your opposition change when you do this. They get agitated and uneasy, and you know then that you have them on the back foot.

You have to be alert for any sign of weakness in your opposition and exploit that weakness. On the other hand, if you have a weakness, be very careful not to show visible signs as those signs are great for someone like me to exploit. The message here is: don't let emotion take control of your body language in a bad situation.

Delivery Preparation

Many questions I am asked by bowlers wanting advice are to do with their delivery action and aiming points. Let's start by concentrating on the draw shot, either forehand or backhand.

Preparation for delivery is the key. Your delivery action should be a result of your preparation. Before you step on the mat what do you do? Think about it.

1.

You should have a good idea of the green speed, which is obviously essential for judging your weight. I normally ask the green keeper what the speed is and where the wind normally comes from. I also ask if any rink is trickier than the others due to a variation in wind conditions. He will also tell you which rinks might have specific imperfections. All this information should be processed and can make a difference in a tight game.

An example of this is when I played at a Gold Coast club where the green on one side was in the shadow of a 30-storey resort building. The wind was blowing from the building end across the green. I asked the green keeper about the wind and he told me that the middle rinks play differently from what you would expect as the wind whips around the building and swirls in a circular motion, requiring a heap more grass on both hands than you would anticipate. He was right. I played against a guy who struggled with his grass for the first half of the game while I was aware of the effect of the wind. Advantage me.

2.

Now that you know the green speed, the direction of the wind
and the effects it will have, before you step onto the mat you
should know what hand you are playing. You shouldn't step
onto the mat until you are clear on this. I'm sure you have seen
heaps of wrong bias bowls put down. Why? The chances are the
bowler was in two minds as to which hand to play. If I am in
two minds, I step back off the mat and start my pre-delivery
again. After you determine which hand to play (and in a team
game the skip in many instances will determine that for you),
run your eyes from the mat to the jack to work out how far the
bowl needs to be delivered. Do this two or three times as it will
help your mind compute what it needs to tell your arm and
body to get the bowl up there. It's very important that all this is
done before you step onto the mat.

3.

Step onto the mat. I won't go into the detail of mat stance and
utilising the mat stance for different shots. Just take up your
stance as shown by your coach.

Again, run your eyes from the mat to the jack. As you take
your stance, you are reinforcing the distance in your mind.

If you are a right-hander, use your right foot as your aiming
foot. It should be pointing directly at the point you need to

deliver your bowl (your grass line). This is very important as this foot is adjusted if you are too wide or too narrow. For left-handers, use your left foot as the aiming foot.

4.

Once your body and feet are facing your delivery point, the focus now becomes the delivery line. This is where many bowlers have been asking for my advice.

I normally choose a point on the bank — the ditch wall or some sort of permanent mark, such as a rink marker or boundary peg, as my aiming point. Whatever you do, don't use a bowls bag or the leg of a seat behind the green as the bag could be moved or somebody could block your view of the seat leg. How many times have you heard a person say, 'Could you step out of the way?' because they can't see their aiming point.

The next thing I do is the important part of my preparation. I bring my eyes from my aiming point (the mark on the bank or rink marker) back to a point ten or twelve feet in front of me. This now becomes my focus and I want to roll my bowl over that point. This is where there are many schools of thought, but for me I find that choosing that point works best and gives me my consistency. By the way, this takes heaps of practice, but once it is part of your routine, bingo — you will achieve the consistency needed to improve your bowls.

My final words here are: practice, practice, practice until it becomes a habit.

4

Delivery Action

I also receive huge numbers of questions about the delivery action, so let's take a look at this.

Let's look firstly at a very short end. I use the elevation method. My bowling arm will be much lower for a short end than a long end, so once I take my stance I determine what position my bowling arm should be compared to the length of the mat to the jack.

Think of your arm as being an hour hand on a clock. No, I'm not going loopy. For instance, when your bowling arm is straight and parallel with the ground, it is what we call the nine o'clock position. Lower the arm slightly to the eight o'clock position and lower again to seven o'clock. Simple!

Coming back to the short end, the speed of the green is also important, of course. My bowling arm is at about the seven o'clock position, then into my delivery action, stepping forward with a smaller step than the longer ends. This step is also very important. Think about this ...

When you walk slowly, you take small steps and your arm swing is minimal. Compare that to a power walk where you take large strides and your arm action is far greater. This comes naturally so we need to take these actions and include them in our delivery.

SHORT ENDS — Lower the bowling arm and take smaller step.

LONG ENDS — Lift the arm higher and take larger step.

The natural swinging action of your bowling arm will give you that consistency we all strive to achieve.

I have seen many bowlers struggle for weight consistency and I notice that their bowling arm is always at the same height, whether it be long or short ends. They obtain their adjustment of weight through the fact that they power their bowling arm from the shoulder rather than allowing the natural momentum of the arm to deliver the bowl.

Again, this requires practice, practice, practice. Have your coach with you to watch and advise, and if you have a video camera get someone to film your delivery action. Have them film at least ten deliveries, so that when you play it back you can see:

a) if you are repetitive with your action,

b) if you are using the elevation method successfully.

A word of advice when practicing your delivery: the draw shot makes up about 85 to 90 percent of your deliveries during a game (leads deliver 100 percent draw shots), so please practice your draw shot. Remember: 85 to 90 percent of the time.

Your Questions Answered

As I mentioned earlier, I want to deal with some of the questions I have received about the game. They are also a reminder for me, because we all need a 'refresh', no matter how experienced we may be. I hope you get something out of these

QUESTION:

I have a problem on slow greens. I use Redlines and I want to know if I can use my positioning on the mat to get more turn out of my bowls.

ANSWER:

Using the mat does not give you extra turn but it does give you a different line. For instance, if I want to play *under* a short bowl that is in my eye on the forehand, I stand as far over to the left of the mat as I legally can (for left-handers, this would be the opposite).

To play *around* a short bowl on my forehand, I move as far to the right of the mat as is legally possible.

As for getting more turn, I have two sets of bowls that I use depending on the speed of the green. I have a tighter line bowl for fast greens and a wider bowl for the slower greens.

Bowls aren't cheap nowadays, so this may not be an option for everyone. The Taylor Redline really is a great all-round bowl, but talk with your coach and discuss this in more detail.

QUESTION:

The bowls I have were my sister in-law's, and I play pretty well with them but still feel they are a little big. Do you believe that the rule 'making the thumbs touch and middle fingers touch' is the best way to go? I cannot do that with the bowls I have.

ANSWER:

All coaches use the measurement of your hand around the bowl as a guide to determine the right size bowl for your use. But there are exceptions to this because some folk may have arthritis of the hand or a differently shaped hand due to a previous injury. If you have reasonable movement of the hand, use this measurement as a guide then borrow a bowl that is the recommended size and have a few rolls to see if it feels comfortable. Some folk make the mistake of getting too big a bowl and eventually their hand and wrist get very sore toward the end of a match. This is because the hand tightens on to the bigger bowl so it won't fall from the hand. Be careful in bowl selection if you intend to put many hours into your bowls. I tend to go smaller than bigger in size as I have more control. Again, I would suggest getting advice from a coach at your club.

QUESTION:

I have trouble holding my size two Edge Plus bowls for long ends on heavy grass greens (running at about 11 to 13 seconds). I am a fairly consistent player and really enjoy fast greens. I use the conventional 'touch grip' and I am wondering if I should change this grip for the claw-type grip or even try a bowls glove? But then would I lose my 'touch'? I have recently changed my bowls from Drakes Special to Edge Plus. My Drakes were size one. The greens in our area are not very good; we have very bad and worn synthetic but also some new synthetic, which is great.

ANSWER:

On a slow green, I prefer to use a palmed bowl. Roll the bowl from your finger tips into your palm so that it sits in the palm of your hand. This will take some practice as it feels so different to the fingertip grip. Deliver as you would normally. The slower the green, the less 'touch' you require so the use of a glove is entirely up to you. The best way is to try it at a practice session and see what works best for you. I have never tried a glove, but I may give it a try one day out of curiosity.

On fast greens that are 14 seconds plus, I sit the bowl on my fingertips. In this position I can really 'feel' the bowl. I know as soon as a bowl leaves my fingertips if it is a good or bad one.

QUESTION:

I find I have trouble playing in windy conditions. I have been bowling wider with the wind and not as wide against the wind. This has helped, but is this the correct method? Can you give me a few tips on how to handle the wind?

ANSWER:

Bowling with the wind and then against the wind the following end is probably the hardest weather condition in which to play as it is like playing on two different greens. With the wind, the bowl runs on, but against the wind it pulls up quickly, so it's very hard to get into a rhythm. I actually like these conditions as I feel I have an advantage over a less experienced opponent who has trouble coming to grips with the conditions. Your green width will vary as bowling against the wind is like playing on a slower green. My main advice is to practise in these conditions. There are no short cuts.

QUESTION:

To push the opponent's bowl away from the jack, do I change my line drawing to the jack? If so, how much do I come inside my line, or what do I do?

ANSWER:

Let's look at a couple of different situations.

Say my opponent's bowl is jack high and he/she is holding shot and I have two seconds behind the jack. In this case, I would draw up to one metre over the head, looking to trail the jack and turn the head from one shot down to two or three shots up.

Let's look at another scenario where my opponent is shot jack high and I have one second jack high on the same side of the head and my opponent has two bowls which are third and fourth shots behind the head. In this case, I would either drive at the jack and ditch it or dead draw. It would be too dangerous to play the one metre over the head shot as I could slice the jack and go three down.

QUESTION:

What are the key ingredients to playing the 'metre on' shot to trail the jack or dislodge a jack high bowl from the head?

ANSWER:

My main tip here is to be very careful not to get too aggressive with this type of shot. I often see players wanting to play a yard over but end up playing two to three metres over. The way I practice this shot is to set up two plastic flip bowls and a flip jack and try to control my weight so that my bowl doesn't end up more than a metre past the head.

I would have to say that this is one of my favourite shots and is one of my strongest for obtaining a conversion during a game.

Practice

Individual Practice Time

When I first started to show signs of having some ability in the game, I was practising between 15 and 25 hours on the green and that was without any real game time. Many bowlers don't realise the commitment needed for practice. Attending the odd practice session is not enough to take you to the top of your game or reach your best ability. If you really want to improve your game, you need to put any spare time into working on your weaknesses and not your strengths.

I see so many people go out on a green, roll up like champions and play one hand only, which is most probably their strongest hand, but under no pressure. But put them in a game and the way they bowl is nothing like how they play in a practice session!

A practice session can be rewarding if you can find a partner who may be a better bowler than yourself, or very keen to improve their game. There is a real benefit in playing some short set-play matches of five or seven ends. By doing this you are practising drawing and running shots, as well as learning different shots that you can play in a match situation. Try one set of short ends and then a set of long ends. It's also a good idea to play two bowl singles as this is good practice if you play fours at any time!

Rolling with a partner will help improve you and your partner's skill levels as long you are both committed to training hard together and not just going out to roll a bowl for the sake of it. However, it is important that you find the time to practise on your own so you can repeat exercises that will improve your weaknesses and consolidate your strengths.

How Does Your Current Practice Routine Rate?

Score one point for each question you answer 'yes' to.

1. Do you usually practise alone?

2. Does your practice session last longer than one hour?

3. Do you use practice worksheets?

4. Does a coach observe your sessions?

5. Do you or your coach plan your practice session before you arrive?

6. Is your practice session structured (i.e. is time allocated for each part)?

7. Do you practise more times each week than you play?

8. Have you used video evaluation to assess your technique?

9. Do you use target grids or tests to measure your practice performance?

10. Do you write down your practice results?

11. Do you include set plays to practise (i.e. place bowls in position at the head)?

12. Do you progressively increase the pressure and/or difficulty of your practice drills?

13. Do you set goals and standards to achieve in practice?

14. Do you have a practised pre-shot routine?

15. Do you enjoy practising bowls?

How did you rate?

10–15 points: Excellent! If you're not already a champion, you soon will be.

5–10 points: Good, but your practice needs to be more frequent and better planned.

0–5 points: You are honest, but most of your practice is probably done using visualisation while at the bar.

Suggested Practice Session

Take around 90 minutes, preferably on your own or with no more than one partner.

This session covers all skills while maintaining emphasis on a good draw shot delivery, but the weighted shots are not neglected. A variety of activities will help maintain interest. If your practice tasks are varied, then repetitive practice need not be tedious or boring.

1.   Activity: Two trial ends, warm up.

     Duration: 10 minutes.

2.   Activity: Delivery draw shot, mat and length the same. Play all bowls up and down the same side. Work on basic delivery style, footwork, swing, line, grassing the bowl and follow through. Follow a pre-shot routine for each delivery. Develop touch and automation.

     Duration: 30 minutes.

3.   Activity: Draw shot variations. Use various mat and jack positions, alternate hands, position bowls, draw to ditch, boundary, etc.

     Duration: 20 minutes.

4.   Activity: Use practice worksheets or set game situations. Develop competitive ability and focus on specific skill (eg. trail shot, short ends with mat up, etc).

Duration: 20 minutes

5. Activity: Weighted shots. Running shots and the drive.

    Duration: 20 minutes.

It is important to have some type of assessment to evaluate your practice. This can be simple or may require more detailed records, as long as they provide some means of comparing your progress. For example, during a set number of ends, count the number of bowls finishing within one metre of the jack, keep score and determine your percentage.

However, remember the purpose and the goals you hope to achieve during each practice session. Keep them in perspective; they are all important, but they only form part of your total development as a player.

Team Practice

I am continually asked for ideas for preparing and practising for pennant or other tournaments involving bowlers in a team and a side game of 'fours', so here goes ...

Your club coaches are the best ones to organise these practice sessions, with the selectors watching on to evaluate individual performances.

1. The coaches should organise all the practice players

onto various rinks with a maximum of eight players per rink and a minimum of four players per rink. Each bowler should have only two bowls and everyone should play a two to four-end roll-up just to get a feel for the green, with the bowls being cleared from the jack after each bowl is rolled.

2. After this warm-up, the coach should split the bowlers into leads, seconds, thirds and skips. Allocate a rink or rinks for the leads to practice on, then rinks for the seconds and so on. It doesn't matter if you have Division 1 leads and Division 3 leads together. This then gives the coach the opportunity to set up a practice session for the leads on their rink/s, the seconds on their rink/s, the thirds on their rink/s and the skips can talk amongst themselves ... only joking!

Leads rink: Set up four jacks on the rink — one short (minimum 23 metres), one long (max length of green) in one direction, and the other two jacks the same in the opposite direction.

Lay the mat close to the 'T' at the beginning of each end. Have each lead bowl two bowls to the short jack (remove two bowls after the player has delivered ready for next bowler), then next end two to the long jack. Have them nominate one side of the green to play, e.g. forehand in one direction then backhand the other direction. Do not allow them to play 'around the clock'. A scoring system should be implemented with points for drawing within a metre, within 30cm and a resting toucher. Each player can record their own scores with the idea of bettering their own score each week.

Seconds rink: At the beginning of each end, set up a head with two bowls sitting jack high either side of the jack (approx 30cm from jack). Vary the length of the mat to jack after each end (short, medium and long). The idea is for the second to play a shot that will outdraw or sit either of the two setup bowls with no more than one metre of weight over the head. Emphasise that they should be over the head and *not* short. A scoring system can be implemented by the coach for each shot, with individual players keeping track of their own score.

Thirds rink: Setup two jacks, one either side of the centre line (one metre max). Have the thirds draw to each jack and allocate points for drawing within one metre, 30cm and resting toucher. In the opposite direction, set up a head with two bowls either side of the jack (approximately 10cm) and play a weighted shot to either remove a bowl or ideally take the jack back. Reset the head after each bowl. The thirds should not loose their bowl in the ditch, the idea being that if they miss the target they still have a live bowl on the green. Allocate points so that the individual bowler has something by which to gauge their personal performance.

Skips Rink: Skips need to practise a range of shots.

First end, set up two bowls in front of the jack (no more than one metre, minimum 30cm) and either side of the centre line as if they are hiding the jack. The idea is to draw around the short bowls for shot. Leave the first bowl on the green then remove both after the second bowl has been delivered.

The second-end setup is to bowl to a displaced jack, with two bowls set up within a metre of the jack with the idea being to draw to beat the other two set-up bowls.

Third end, set up two bowls on either side of the jack (approximately 10cm) and drive at the bowls and jack, ideally taking the jack back into the ditch.

Fourth end, set up two bowls on either side of the jack (approximately 30cm from jack) and play a shot that will outdraw or sit either of the two setup bowls with no more than one metre of weight over the head.

Repeat the process from the first end again, making sure you have a scoring system in place so that each bowler can gauge their performance.

3. To finish the practice session, coach and selectors should divide all players into the regular playing teams, or the teams that may end up playing together. This gives selectors an opportunity to

sort out compatibility issues and to try to grade the players and teams in a two-to-five-end shoot out.

I recently came across a new training tool called the Rebound Disc Practice System. It is actually coloured rubber discs that replicate bowls and jack that are fixed to the green and rebound after the bowl passes over them. It is great for practicing weighted shots as well as draw shots. It enables you to set up a variety of different heads and saves time by not having to reposition bowls or other training objects after the bowl passes over. I have been so impressed with this development as a beneficial training and coaching aid that I have agreed to support it. If you want to assess it for yourself, I suggest you go to www.rebounddisc.com.au

Most important is that a practice session is planned and organised, otherwise nothing will be achieved except for having a rollup with your mates …

I hope this helps you and your team mates. There are many variations that you could also introduce to your team practice … go for it!

6

Psychology in Bowls

Many people ask me about the 'mental' side of this great game of lawn bowls and how I prepare for a big game. I don't want to give away all my secrets ... only joking!

Let's look at the 'psychology' of lawn bowls, but first let me say that I don't have a major preparation for a game these days. To be honest, I have played so many top games against some fantastic bowlers that another BIG game doesn't faze me and I don't get that nervous. I guess I am lucky in that respect because when I talk to some of the other top bowlers they tell me they do get very nervous before a big game.

Most coaches will tell you that to become a great bowler, 20 percent lies in technique and 80 percent is psychology. I think it is even more than that: it's 10 percent technique and 90 percent psychology.

I have total confidence in my delivery because I practise so much, so in competition I concentrate on my inner belief system. It may sound weird, but when I am ready to bowl I know exactly what I want to do and I convince myself that the shot I want to play will happen.

When I first started bowling, it was nearly impossible to convince myself that I could deliver the bowl exactly as I wanted because one part of me was saying, 'Hey, that shot is very difficult and I might not even get close.' It wasn't until I had played many top level games that my belief system kicked in.

I reflected on previous games in my mind and on a particular shot that I had played well and simply said to myself, 'Hey, play the same shot again.' I knew I could do it.

Let me ask you this question: 'Do you ever doubt yourself in the shot you are about to play?' If you answer 'yes', you have to overcome this and be able to truly believe in yourself and the shot you can make. It isn't easy and only comes with playing more top-level games. I have to tell you that if your belief system is not up to scratch, you will let yourself down! Guess what: if you don't believe you can do it, most often you will succeed in not doing it!

There is a whole lot more to the psychology of the game, but one of the most important ingredients to achieving better results is your fitness.

Your mum and dad probably told you this as a child (and you have more than likely said it to your own children or grandchildren): 'Fit body, fit mind.' Please do me a favour: take that first step and get fit (if you aren't already). I don't mean that you need a six-pack stomach, but you do need to be just fit enough to have the mental alertness that may help you take your bowls to the next level.

7

Advice for New Bowlers

When you first begin this great sport of lawn bowls, you can have coaching lessons, get advice from well-intentioned friends and experienced bowlers, read books, or even watch televised bowls. However, regardless of the advice you are able to gather, lawn bowls really is a game of line, length, and luck.

Fact is, bowls is a game of primitive origins. Archaeologists claim to have found cave drawings, supposedly from the Ice Age, which depict men rolling a large rock towards a smaller rock.

There is no right or wrong way to play this game, but there is a way in which you can be comfortable and which works for you consistently. That's the key word: consistency!

It is then a coach's job to fine-tune that delivery, to make it almost 'mechanical', and then it comes down to your work ethic or dedication to perfect the delivery. The sooner you can deliver every bowl the same, the sooner you will start to achieve whatever results you might be aspiring to.

To achieve the correct line, it is best to use a straight line as your aiming line.

By this I mean using a reference point on the bank, such as a boundary peg, and bowling along this line. This is much easier than using the imaginary curved line many top bowlers use, which is difficult to remember and correct.

New players who are having problems with consistent line and length should follow these tips:

- Practise on your own.

- Place a jack on the centre line to the length you wish to practise.

- Place another jack along your aiming line parallel to the jack on the centre line.

- Deliver your bowl looking directly along the line to the jack on your aiming line. This gives you the weight and the line for a draw shot to the jack on the centre line.

- Play with just two bowls and walk up and replay the bowls from the same end and same hand until you become comfortable with the system, then change to the other hand.

- Remember this is only one method for finding your line. You need to alter or fine-tune a method so that you are comfortable with it and it works for you.

8

Team Play

The Lead

Each of you will play as either a lead, second, third or skip at some time, so you may find this information useful.

Firstly, I want to pass on some success-proven advice for bowlers playing in the lead position. The position of lead in any team is extremely important as it is a platform to the team's success. Many bowlers believe that it is the most menial position in a team, but nothing could be further from the truth. I know when I accept an invitation to skip a rink, my first thought is: 'Who will I get to lead?'

A top-class lead must be dedicated, as they very rarely see their name in lights or receive the accolades they deserve. The lead attempts to deliver the jack to where the skip requires it. Very few people, however, practice rolling the jack, and this is a major requirement of a good lead.

Sometimes a skip may ask for a jack to be delivered to a length the lead is not playing well to, but that the team is gaining shots at. If the lead delivers to the skip's required length, they are still playing an important part in winning the game.

Here are a few basic rules for leads:

- A lead's job is to establish a foundation on which the team can build a winning head. The duty of a lead is to place their two bowls as close to the jack as possible. The old classic phrase of 'one on and one behind' is great in theory, but extremely difficult in practice. However, if you can place your two bowls consistently within a yard of the jack, you will please even the most demanding skip.

- The lead is *not* playing singles against their opposing lead. If the opposition draws a resting toucher, their job is *not* to dislodge that bowl, but to draw as close to it as possible with both bowls. If you attempt to shift a close opposition bowl, you are no longer playing lead, and your bowls will not finish close to the jack. Look around on social days and observe the undisciplined leads; they often have a compulsion to 'niggle' at the shot bowl or jack and leave their team vulnerable and without close bowls in the head.

- Do not change hands unnecessarily. Find the kindest hand in each direction, which is usually on the same side of the green, and stick to it. Even if you or the opposition place a short bowl that is in the way, stick to the hand you know as you can draw around or under the short bowl by correcting your grass. Every time you change your hand, you force yourself into playing a new shot and are less likely to gain consistency.

- When playing away from your home club, take particular notice what hand the opposing lead is playing as the local players will know which hands are the kindest. Use their knowledge.

- Concentrate on delivering the jack as close to your skip's direction as you can; many games have been lost by badly delivered jacks. Correct delivery of the jack is just as important to the team as a toucher, so give it the same concentration and commitment.

- The lead is essential to the team's chances of playing well. In most instances you will notice that if the lead plays well, the team plays well, and conversely if the lead struggles, the team struggles.

The Second

We often hear old stagers joke that the main responsibility of a good second is to provide a neat scorecard and keep the scoreboard up to date — and it is exactly that: a joke.

It is sometimes wrongly perceived that the second can be the weak link in a fours team — the position in which you can put any player no matter what their ability. Again, this is a perception that is totally false. In most good skippers' opinion, the second is judged to be important in a team, and a position that requires the services of a specialist.

A good second is a player who allows the team to build the head, gives the team a foundation to build from, is able to consolidate when the lead plays two good bowls, and can retrieve the situation when the lead fails.

It is usually only after the second's bowls have been played that the skipper determines whether to call positive attacking shots, or whether to be careful and defensive with the remaining bowls to be played.

If your lead and second are out-bowling their opposition, in most instances you should win the game. This is because it allows the third and skip to play positional bowls when holding the shot, while also giving them the opportunity to attack or play positive bowls when the team is down on the head. It is also much easier to draw a shot if you are already holding the shot.

The second's main shots — the ones which should be practiced with regularity and repetition to become a specialist — are the draw and the 'yard-on' shot.

If your team is holding shot, be just behind the head; if your team is down, draw or just arrive with a minimum of weight so that your bowl remains in the head. The main aim is to consolidate or retrieve the shot.

Here are the priorities of a good second:

- To be no worse than one down after playing your bowls.

- Don't get on the mat until you have been given directions.

- Don't get on the mat with your own preconceived shot in mind.

- When given a shot to play, play that shot with total commitment and belief, even if you disagree with the instruction.

- Hand your team-mates their bowls along with a word of encouragement or praise.

- Give 100 percent commitment to the skipper and the team.

- *Never* have both of your bowls *short* of the jack.

The Third

The third is the skipper's assistant, the second in charge, the communicator between the skip and the team, the team motivator. The third must be able to ensure loyalty and support from the other players to the team and the skip. They should always be aware of any changes or opportunities that may present themselves while in control of the head.

The third's job is to advise the skip on what shots are available and, if asked, what shot to play. The third should always be aware of the position of every bowl in the head and where any danger may exist, as well as knowing the skip's strengths and weaknesses. They should call the shot that suits the skip's type of game and what the skip can play, and not what they themselves can play.

Try during the game to analyse the opposing skip's game, their strengths and weaknesses, on which hand they draw best, on which hand they drive best, etc. It will be very advantageous towards the end of the game to be able to advise the skip on what shot to play if you have a fair idea of what shot the opposing skip will play and his chances of success.

A good third is a person who is very proficient in all the range of shots, is a good measurer, is able to ensure the continued motivation and commitment of the players to the team's success, and has the respect and trust of the skip when in control of the head.

When drawing counters to the shot, always try to count by drawing wide. For instance, if the second shot is 500mm away, try to count by drawing 400mm wide or jack high. Nothing saps the lead and second's confidence more than holding the shot only to see it given away by their own players. Likewise, a positional bowl is just as important as a resting toucher, so play it with the same concentration and commitment.

When the skip asks you for an opinion, your job is to advise them of the shot options available to them. The decision on what shot they prefer to play is their choice, not yours, unless they ask you specifically, 'What do you want?'

The Skipper

The skipper does not have to be the best player in the team but he or she should be a natural leader, motivator and psychologist, able to inspire commitment and dedication in the team, and most importantly, must be a good tactician. He or she must be able to direct the team with confidence, play them to their individual strengths, while also having the ability to analyse the opposition's strengths and weaknesses.

The skip should be able to create calm and confidence in the team by the way he moves around the head and calls the shots, without panic, disappointment or appearing flustered while under pressure. The best way to get people to play better is to give them encouragement and confidence. A good skip is one who can encourage a player who has begun the game badly into playing better before the game finishes.

I can't stress enough the importance of calling the players to their individual strengths. If the obvious shot is not one of the players' strengths, call some other shot they have a good chance of playing, and leave the obvious shot to another player. It is bad skipping and a poor percentage play when you call shots with a very low success rate.

When giving difficult shot directions to the players, it is most important that you watch their faces as this will give you a good indication of the players consent. By watching the expression on the players face or the body language given, the skip will usually be able to tell:

a)   if the player can see the shot that is being called,

b) whether or not the player shows the confidence to play the shot.

If a player looks unsure about the shot, or is not confident of playing the shot, it is pointless to ask them to play it as their chance of success is low.

You have two options in this case:

a) You bring them up to the head, and discuss the shot you want them to play.

b) You change the shot to one that they are capable and confident of playing.

Never forget this old and very true saying: 'If you think you can't, you won't!'

The skip should involve the players in the decisions and tactics of the game whenever possible. The best way to get support and commitment from the team is to communicate with the players during the change-over and let them know what you are trying to do. How often have you heard a member of a team say, 'What is he/she going to play?' being answered with, 'I haven't got a clue'? When giving directions to the players, place your hand or foot where you want the bowl to finish. This will assist the player in choosing the correct line and weight.

When you are multiple shots down on the head, and trying to draw to save, always play the hand that *you* have the most confidence in drawing close, and not what may look to others the obvious way to get the absolute shot. When drawing another shot, always try to draw jack high to beat the opposition's closest bowl. Do not cross the centre line, so that if you are heavy you pass the head on the outside and you don't give the shot away.

There is usually 15 percent luck in most games. To get lucky you need to be 'up' with your bowls.

When you are down on the head, remember these rules:

- You can't roll bowls up, get wicks, sit bowls or trail jacks, unless you have weight to reach the jack.

- Luck doesn't happen in bowls unless you pass the jack.

When you are considering the choice of shot to play, consider the following:

- What is the ability of the player to be able to play the shot?

- What does the team gain by playing the shot?

- What does the team stand to lose if the shot goes wrong?

- What are the chances of the shot going wrong?

- What is the absolute worst that can happen?

- Is this the right time in the match to play this shot?

- Can I retrieve the situation if things go wrong?

A good skip will have self-discipline, a calm temperament, and will always appear to be in control of the situation. They will appear cool, with constructive thoughts, even when under extreme pressure. They will play to a plan when in trouble, and endeavour to lose the least amount of shots per end.

When things get tight, they will consider only relevant factors, take their time, and be positive in the decisions they give. Be aware of the changing conditions and play the correct tactical game for those conditions. Communicate with the team at all times so that everyone is aware of what the objectives are. This will help in the commitment and team spirit of those concerned, and assist in the goal of building a champion team.

If you talk, think, and act positive thoughts, your bowls will reflect those images.

Now, finally, I'm going to say this one more time:

CONCENTRATION and **CORRECTION** gives **CONSISTENCY.**

COMPATIBILITY and **COMMITMENT** makes **CHAMPIONS.**

Good Bowling,
Kelvin Kerkow

Major Bowls Achievements

KELVIN KERKOW
MAJOR BOWLS ACHIEVEMENTS

International

Pacific Games Singles Gold Medallist 1995

World Bowls Singles and Triples Bronze Medal 1996

Pacific Games Singles and Triples Silver Medal 1997

Burnside Invitational Pairs Winner, New Zealand 1998

World Bowls Silver Medal 2004

Scottish International Open Winner 2006

World Indoor Bowls Pairs Champion 1996, 2005, 2009

Welsh Masters Invitational Singles Champion 1997, 2005, 2006

Commonwealth Games Singles Gold Medal 2006

Country and Queensland Titles

State Junior Singles Champion 1986

State Pairs Champion 1994, 1999, 2001, 2007, 2008

State Fours Champion 1995, 1997, 2006, 2009

State Singles Champion 1995

Australian Fours Champion 1995, 1997

Queensland State Player of the Year 2000, 2001, 2003, 2006

Australian Indoor Champion 2006, 2007

Australian Representative   1995-2008

Queensland Representative   1989-2009

Other Major Tournament Successes

Gold Coast Winter Carnival Fours 1988, 1999

Hub of the Hunter Invitation Singles 1992

Coolangatta Master of Masters 1993

Golden Nugget Invitation Singles 1994, 1997, 2008

Gold Coast Winter Carnival Singles 1996

Noosa Invitational Pairs 1997

Gold Coast Winter Carnival Pairs 1997

Sandgate Easter Open Singles 1997

Ballina Summerland Singles 1999

Mount Isa Invitational Singles 1989, 1999, 2001

Halekulani Invitation Singles 1999

Logan City Master Pairs 1999, 2000

Mount Isa Invitation Singles 2000

Springwood Invitation Fours 2000

Gold Coast Champion of Champion Singles and Pairs 2000

Gold Coast Winter Carnival Fours and Mixed Triples 2000

Banora Point Invitation Fours 2000

Port Macquarie Invitation Singles 2000

Mount Gravatt Open Pairs 2000

Lismore Invitation Fours 2000

Bribie Island Open Singles 1994, 2000, 2003

Mount Isa Invitation Singles Winner 2001

Gold Coast Champion of Champion Fours 2001

Tweed Heads Energex Open Singles Winner 2001

A SPECIAL THANK YOU

To everyone who has supported me over the years...
whether playing for Australia, Queensland, my Club or
other tournaments...your encouragement has helped
me get over the line on many occasions. A special
thank you to my family, friends and spectators who
cheered me on at the Commonwealth Games gold
medal game in 2006 at Darebin in Melbourne! You
made all the difference! To my State and Australian
team members and International team mates...i have
enjoyed playing with each and every one of you and
thank you for your support over the years. Thank you
also to my past Clubs, and to my present Club, South
Tweed, i am extremely grateful for your support.